Mindfulness for Students

www.palgravestudyskills.com – the leading study skills website

Palgrave Study Skills

For a complete listing of all our titles in this area please visit **macmillanihe.com/study-skills**

Mindfulness for Students

Stella Cottrell

 macmillan education   palgrave

First published 2018 by
PALGRAVE

Palgrave in the UK is an imprint of Macmillan Publishers Limited, registered in England, company number 785998, of 4 Crinan Street, London, N1 9XW.

Palgrave® and Macmillan® are registered trademarks in the United States, the United Kingdom, Europe and other countries.

ISBN 978–1–352–00235–5 paperback

This book is printed on paper suitable for recycling and made from fully managed and sustained forest sources. Logging, pulping and manufacturing processes are expected to conform to the environmental regulations of the country of origin.

A catalogue record for this book is available from the British Library.

A catalog record for this book is available from the Library of Congress.

Printed and bound in the UK by Bell and Bain Ltd, Glasgow.

Contents

List of Guided Exercises

Foreword

Student life can already be so pressurized that it might seem as if learning about mindfulness, and dedicating time to it every day, is just too much. My own experience of being a student was that the opposite was true: mindfulness practice really helped.

In the 1990s, I became a student again. Although I already had a PhD, I decided to enroll for a BSc (Honours) degree in Psychology with the Open University and to complete this in just two years. I was also working full time, writing a book, and I was on a national working party improving support arrangements for students with dyslexia. With so much to do, I was racing from pillar to post, buzzing with ideas, talking at high speed. I had to get everything done – fast. Friends and colleagues asked me politely to slow down a little, or maybe just finish my sentences off occasionally when talking. (They still do, sometimes.)

It might not appear to have been a good time for me to start yet another course, but I noticed an advert for meditation classes in Royal Oak in West London. I was curious although deeply suspicious, not really knowing what meditation was and wondering what I might be letting myself in for. However, I acknowledged that maybe I could do with a little more calm in my life, so off I went, to find out more and give it a go.

Once a week, I travelled for over an hour each way across London to get to class. It was friendly and clear. There was no pressure. The world didn't turn upside down. I wasn't suddenly a different person. But, I knew from early on that if I kept practising, this would do me good. I wished I had learnt about mindfulness, Metta and 'skilful and unskilful thinking' whilst at school! When the course ended, I found other classes and groups, attending these twice a week or more. It was worth it, and I still found time to do everything else.

I achieved a 'first class' for my degree and a Bruner prize that the Open University awarded to the highest achievers on the Psychology degree. I mention this not to boast, but to indicate what can be achieved even when it seems 'there is no time'. Mindfulness practice made a big difference to me when studying, enriched my life, and made me a better person than I would have been otherwise. I hope this now helps others.

Stella Cottrell

Acknowledgements

For this book, I have drawn heavily on a wide range of writings and research, but especially on my own training from others and of others. In particular, I am grateful for my introduction to Mindfulness of Breathing and Metta Bhavana meditation practices by Sarvabhadri at classes in the West London Buddhist Centre in the early 1990s. Sarvabhadri was inspiring in her manner and speech, demonstrating the effects of mindfulness in simple everyday interaction. I am grateful for the many years of teaching, talks and shared practice I gained subsequently, primarily through the London Buddhist Centre, as well as at Taraloka, Dhanakosa and elsewhere.

In working with students, in my previous books and now here, I have drawn on the experiences and insights gained from well over two decades of mindfulness practice. I am grateful to students who had a go at different ways of doing things, including trying out meditation, and for sharing their experiences. There are too many to name individually.

There has been a great surge in research into the efficacy of mindfulness practice – where I have drawn on this, it is acknowledged in the text. I would also like to offer my thanks to the many others who didn't get named but whose work also forms part of the backdrop of our developing understanding of an area where it can be difficult to tie down results that are 'measurable' whilst also meaningful to the experience.

As always, I am immensely grateful to the staff at Palgrave who have encouraged me to write this book and who work so hard to produce it. Special thanks to Georgia Park, Rosie Maher and Jocelyn Stockley, who have contributed to the production of this edition.

A very special thank you to Suzannah Burywood, Helen Caunce and Claire Dorer who are immense sources of inspiration and motivation, and without whom this book would not have happened.

The beauty of mindfulness

It is simple.

It can be challenging, subtle, nuanced, rewarding.

It can be a solitary or a shared activity.

It can bring unexpected insights, experiences, clarity, balance and contentment – often when least expected.

You can practise it anytime, anywhere.

You can practise it as much or as little as you like.

Even a little mindfulness goes a long way. The longer you stick with it, the more you benefit.

It is a route to enhancing inner resources that can benefit you across your lifetime, in any context.

You can apply it to any aspect of your life.

It can be life-transforming.

And it doesn't need to cost anything.

Introduction

Are you open to a different approach to study?

What if your study was a pleasure, not a struggle nor something just to 'get through' to gain the qualification?

What if study absorbed your attention, stimulated your mind, and brought a sense of contentment in time well spent?

What if you felt calm and composed about what you are able to accomplish, maintaining a balanced perspective and sense of well-being?

What if you were able to manage study-related anxiety, feeling more in control of your study and its outcomes?

If you already love your course and focus your attention effectively whenever you study, if you don't get stressed or anxious, if you keep your study goals in perspective, and maintain a sense of well-being and mental serenity, then it sounds as if you have already found a great recipe for learning and for life.

Otherwise, if you would like your studies to be more like that, then this book could be for you. To benefit from it, you just need to be open to:

~ Experiencing greater calm and balance

~ Trying out the techniques for yourself

~ Practising them, to experience the greatest benefit

~ Enjoying the process.

What you can gain from this book

This book draws on ancient ways of being, doing and thinking that have been practised by millions of people for over 2500 years. These have been passed down largely from one set of practitioners to another and are now used in a wide range of contexts around the world to bring benefits to study, life, health and well-being. The book provides you with the following.

Background – so you understand, broadly, what mindfulness is; its origins, and the benefits when applied to life and study now.

Techniques – that you can learn and apply to specific study contexts and in everyday life.

Practical guidance on applying mindfulness to study – so you can draw on mindfulness when engaged in a range of study tasks, from listening in lectures, to reading and writing for assignments, preparing for exams, and managing the stresses of student life.

Research findings – to provide context on the efficacy and benefits of mindfulness techniques, as well as information on related areas such as attention and multi-tasking. Findings are provided in summary so you can grasp the headlines and consider the implications for your own study. Although there is a great deal of research, much is relatively new, so the landscape of what is understood may change over time.

Guided observations – to develop your awareness, or mindfulness, of your approach to study.

Structured reflections – to help refine your practice and integrate mindfulness into your study habits, thinking processes and everyday life.

Prompt sheets and templates – to help structure and record your reflections and time spent in mindful activity. These aren't an essential part of mindfulness practice but can help.

Tips and FAQs – to help address common questions that face beginners.

This book isn't a standard study skills book. There are other books that provide those skills (see page xxii). Instead, it focuses on how you can draw on mindfulness as an alternative, or complementary, way to approach study.

How to use this Book

Mindfulness for Students has been designed as an easy-to-use, practical guide. It includes contextual information to provide a solid foundation for your practice and ground your understanding. There are no hard and fast rules about which order to do things: you can work through the chapters in the order they appear, or you may prefer to gain a taste of each Part, moving around the book selectively to suit your interests, study needs and level of prior experience. It is likely that you will find the book of most benefit if you do the following.

1. Find out what to expect

Check out what mindfulness is, where it originated, why it is becoming so popular and how it works. It is recommended that you do begin with the 'Pause the world' activity in Chapter 1. After that, browse Part 1, reading any chapters that look useful for you or capture your interest in the first instance.

2. Have a go

To fully understand 'mindfulness' you need to experience it. You can begin with just a few minutes of a starter exercise to gain an initial sense of what might be involved. It isn't difficult to get going, and Part 2, *Techniques*, provides step-by-step guidance.

- If you haven't much experience of meditation already, the logical place to begin is the *Starter Exercises* (Chapters 13–17).
- If you are already familiar with meditation, you may like to move forward to meditations or applications that are new to you.
- When you are ready, learn the meditations of Mindfulness of Breathing (Chapters 18 and 19) and Metta (Chapter 21).

You don't have to complete all the Techniques before you can apply them to your studies and life.

3. Use it

Browse Part 3, *Applying Mindfulness to Study*, to gain a sense of why and how mindfulness will be useful to your own study. The opening chapters are of general relevance and underpin other chapters in this section. Select the most relevant chapters for you now and apply the guidance there alongside what you are discovering from practical techniques covered in Part 2. Select other chapters in Part 3 when these become relevant to your study circumstances.

4. Gain the benefits

Traditionally, practitioners of 'mindfulness' benefited and learnt from their experience by engaging with it – by establishing a regular practice, observing what happened, thinking about it afterwards, discussing it, and applying it to their life. It is up to you how much, or how little, you engage with mindfulness practice, using the materials and resources provided in this book.

~ On the benefits of mindfulness, see Chapters 8 and 9 and the relevant chapters in Part 3.

~ On observations and reflections, see page xxi and Part 4.

~ On establishing a regular practice, see Chapter 23.

~ On applying meditation to your study, see Part 3.

~ On meditating with others, see Chapter 24.

~ On applying meditation to everyday life, see Chapters 22, 25 and 26.

Experiencing stress, anxiety or mental ill-health?

'Mindfulness' approaches and practice have been found to be helpful for bringing a sense of calm when stressed; see Chapter 46 for further detail about mindfulness in the context of stresses typically associated with study. If you are experiencing high levels of stress and anxiety, have a history of mental ill-health, or think you might be clinically depressed or going through a difficult time, do take note of pages 22 and 40. It is sensible to have the right support in place before starting a meditation practice.

About the four sections

Part 1. *What is mindfulness?*

Part 1 provides an introduction to 'Mindfulness' and meditation so that you can consider whether this approach is right for you. Although the basic steps are very simple, the application and experience are different for each individual. This section introduces research into the benefits of mindfulness practice in general and for students. It considers myths and misconceptions that sometimes surround mindfulness, the potential downsides as well as the benefits, so that you have a more rounded view of what it entails in the context of student life.

Part 2. *Techniques*

This section provides easy-to-follow guidance on mindfulness meditations, related concepts and everyday applications. These give you a good foundation for developing 'mindfulness' in ways that have deeper and longer-lasting benefits. It begins with short exercises to familiarize you with what is involved in mindfulness meditation; it is useful to return to these exercises occasionally to remind you of the basics and to strengthen the foundations of your practice. Part 2 also looks at developing a personal mindfulness practice, preparing and setting up your sessions well, and dealing with typical challenges. Managing such challenges is an important and integral part of developing 'mindfulness'.

Part 3. *Applying mindfulness to study*

'Mindfulness', as the word suggests, brings us back continually to what is going on in our minds, and how that affects the way we approach whatever we are doing or that arises for us. This section gives you the opportunity to explore certain key thought patterns that are associated with traditional mindfulness practice, applied here to study tasks and contexts. These include a consideration of how basic core emotions and thought patterns associated with wanting and not-wanting, 'craving' and 'aversion', can have a powerful effect on whether we approach study skilfully or, alternatively, delude us into unhelpful responses and habits.

Part 3 looks at research into concentration, attention and task-switching, considering the impact of mindful practice on effective study. It provides guidance on applying mindfulness to typical study tasks such as reading, writing, listening, using feedback and preparing for exams, and to typical aspects of student life, such as studying alone and in class, managing time and dealing with stress and anxiety.

Part 4. *Records and reflections*

The final Part includes a brief introduction to reflection and record-keeping in the context of 'mindfulness'. This section consists primarily of resources that you can draw on, as and when you wish, to assist you in keeping a record of your practice. These resources are also available on the companion website. If you would like to keep track of your activities in developing mindfulness, see pages 195–6.

↖ Companion website

A companion website for the book is available at www.macmillanihe.com/mindfulness
This contains:

~ audio versions of selected exercises and meditations

~ templates of materials in Part 4, for your personal use.

Symbols used in the book

Observation

Reflection

Meditation or Guided Exercise

Self-Evaluation

Companion Website: item available on the companion website for personal use

Observations, reflections and record-keeping

Use structured observations, reflections and activities

You will find that, over time, pausing to observe, record, and reflect on what you notice, will help you to focus attention and gain insights (see Chapter 47).

- ~ Guided observations, reflections and prompts are provided throughout the chapters as well as in Part 4. It is recommended that you complete at least some of these, to sharpen your focus, extend your observation and deepen your thinking.

- ~ You don't have to do every reflection or answer every question: select those that strike a chord with you or stimulate your interest.

When to focus? When to reflect?

During mindfulness exercises and meditations, just be receptive to the experience as it arises. Let yourself focus on the object of the exercise or meditation without becoming diverted into making sense of it at the time. Don't stop at this point to analyse, interpret or take down notes.

Later, perhaps a few minutes after you have completed a meditation, reflect on it and anything that arose that seems important or interesting.

It is also useful to pause and reflect occasionally on how your attitude, practice and study habits are changing over time. See Part 4.

Keeping a record

You don't need to note anything down in order to be mindful, but you may be glad later on if you do jot down your observations and thoughts. These can help to clarify your thinking at the time. It also means you can look back and observe how your thinking and experience develop with time. Your record could be visual or as audio rather than as written notes, if you prefer.

Part 4 contains templates that you can copy and use to record details of your practice and reflections, if you wish. These can also be downloaded from the companion website (see page xx).

Complementary books for study skills

This book complements rather than replaces books about study skills. It looks at how mindfulness can help and enhance study rather than taking you step by step through the processes of adapting to student life or completing specific kinds of study tasks. If you feel you would benefit from improving your study skills, I have written several titles that you may find useful such as those below. Full details of these can be found in the References on pages 207–8.

The Study Skills Handbook – this covers a range of skills and approaches, step by step. It is used at all levels of study, and is ideal when starting a new course, starting at university, or for refreshing your skills after a gap year or break.

The Palgrave Student Planner – this is updated every year, to help you keep track of all those things that you need to remember and organize as a student.

Skills for Success: Personal Development and Employability – this looks at study success in the round, considering your values, inspiration, personal approaches to enhancing performance, as well as generic skills such as creative thinking, people skills, reflective practice and employability awareness. All these assist both study and work.

Critical Thinking Skills – an in-depth look at criticality, as an essential skill for life and for higher-level study. This provides a step-by-step approach with lots of practice opportunities.

The Exam Skills Handbook: Achieving Peak Performance – this looks at how to approach exams as if you were an athlete, developing focused expertise.

Dissertations and Project Reports – a step-by-step guide to make longer assignments more manageable.

Part 1

What is mindfulness?

1

Mindfulness as experience

Pause the world for a moment ...

Imagine you could press a button to slow down or stop the world around you. In this stiller world, you could take in your experience with greater awareness. As a result, you could then have more control over how you responded to whatever happened, minute-by-minute. What would that be like?

Below, you will be invited to do that before reading further. You may prefer to keep reading instead, but if you stick with the task, it will help you to make more sense of what you read later.

Activity: Pause the world ...

Take a few moments to imagine a situation where, by slowing down the world, you have the opportunity to do something differently. Consider what that would be like. **Before getting started**, take a few moments to consider your response to being asked to undertake this activity. Use the prompts below to assist your observations and to explore your response. You can come back to the activity on page 7 (below).

Prompts for 'Pause the world'	
How do you feel about what you have been asked to do?	Interested? Keen to give this a go? Irritated? Impatient to get on with reading? Reluctant? Resistant? Something else? Don't know?
Are you judging your responses?	Are you pleased with yourself for having a great attitude? Blaming yourself for being impatient or adopting a negative attitude? Defensive about your attitude? Wary that your response to this activity may be criticized? Or not judging at all?
What about your emotions?	Are you aware of any other emotions, or feelings, at this moment? Happiness? Contentment? Sadness? Anger? Anxiety? Joy? Serenity? Worry? Shame? Guilt? Defensiveness? No feelings at all?
	What does it feel like to have such feelings: good? Uncomfortable? Don't know? Do you have a sense of trying to avoid any particular feelings and emotions just now?
What do you notice about your body?	Do you feel comfortable? Uncomfortable? Relaxed? Tense? Peaceful? Stiff? Painful? Itchy? Upright? Happy to be sitting still or keen to be getting up and doing something else? Or are you not really aware of your body? Don't know? Don't want to know?

Interpreting your responses to the prompts

The above prompts were designed …

~ To encourage you to bring your attention to what, exactly, was going on for you at that moment

~ To bring your attention to your feelings, thoughts and physical responses, increasing your awareness of these

~ To deepen your experience of the present moment more fully, whether that was pleasant or annoying – to just 'be' with whatever came up.

Being observant of the here and now

Mindfulness starts with being more fully aware of what is going on, starting with your own mind and body. As you worked through the prompts, you may have noticed some or all of the following:

1. That you went through a train of different thoughts and emotions

2. That your thoughts and emotions changed as you read the prompts, responding to each of these as a new stimulus

3. That you wanted to 'get on with it', to read on rather than pause to increase your awareness of what was going on in the moment

4. That you wanted to have the 'right' response – to be 'good at' whatever this was supposed to be about

5. That you wondered if you had 'got it wrong', maybe getting anxious or annoyed about this or about being 'judged'

6. That you were quick to start judging yourself, maybe praising yourself, maybe criticizing yourself negatively

7. That you couldn't really be bothered to engage with some or all of the prompts, or that some interested you more than others

8. That you didn't know how to answer some

9. That even though nobody but you would know how you responded, you were not entirely honest, or invented responses

10. That your response was primarily intellectual: you were already starting to formulate theories, arguments, objections, criticisms.

Gaining insights

As you may have guessed, there are not any correct or incorrect responses to the prompts. You aren't 'good' or 'bad' as a result of your responses. They may give you insights into such things as:

- How open and willing you are to 'have a go' and participate
- The sorts of things to which you find it easy or difficult to respond with equanimity, balance and calm
- The kinds of things you are quick to criticize or push away
- Your levels of self-criticism and sensitivity to being judged
- Your awareness of your body, thoughts, and/or emotions.

▲ Reflection: Awareness of experience

- Take a few moments to jot down your observations and reflections on this activity.
- From the list of 10 sets of responses itemized above (page 5), which ones did you observe yourself engaging in at some point during the activity?
- What might you learn about yourself from these observations?

Mindfulness as experience

You can read about mindfulness and, indeed, there are many excellent and thought-provoking writings that you can draw upon to enhance, understand or critique the experience. However, reading and hearing about mindfulness only takes you so far. Considering research findings only takes you so far. The experience is different: you find out for yourself. Mindfulness practice brings depth and breadth to your experience, to the practice itself and to your life and studies more generally.

If you followed through on the activity, responding to the prompts above, you are starting to experience what mindfulness is about. You do it. You experience. You observe. You learn.

The power of the pause

You can be mindful, or more aware, at any time, whether you are in stillness or undertaking an activity. However, the thought patterns, habits, abilities and benefits associated with mindfulness are usually developed through setting time aside just to pause, focus, notice, practice.

Creating such pauses increases your awareness of what is going on for you in the immediacy of the here and now:

- Of your surroundings
- Of your physical self
- Of your feelings, cravings, aversions, emotions
- Of inner chatter, trains of thought, responses, reactions to responses, whether you are judging yourself or being kind to yourself, judging others or bringing empathetic compassion to their circumstances
- Of whatever is arising in your mind and what this leads you to think, feel, do, or want to do, in the immediate moment.

⬥ Reflection: Pause the world for a moment ...

Reflect now on the paragraph with which this chapter opened.

Imagine you could press a button to slow down or stop the world around you. In this stiller world, you could take in your experience with greater awareness. It would give you more control over how you responded to whatever happened, moment-by-moment.

- What would that be like?
- What kinds of things might you do differently?
- What might you learn?
- How might your life and your studies be different as a result?
- What would it be like if everyone did this?

Shaping your experience

Although we do not have control over all aspects of our existence, we do have a great deal of power over how we experience it. There is a lot of power in our own minds – much more than we usually employ.

However wonderful or terrible an experience, we can shape how we think and feel about it to some extent:

- by the way we think about it
- by the way we talk about it
- by what we do to prepare mentally and physically in advance
- by how open and active we are in learning from it
- by the way we set up a task for success or failure
- by how we organize our surroundings
- by our choice of who we involve in what we do
- by taking action
- by drawing on our observations
- by reflecting on our actions
- by how we refine and apply our awareness.

For students, this is relevant because it means you can influence how you experience your own study. This is picked up further in Chapter 32, 'Finding the joy in study'.

It is also relevant to mindfulness practice itself. When meditating, although it isn't helpful to try to tie down a particular experience, you can influence the experience through the way you set up your practice. This is considered further in Chapter 23, 'Developing your practice'.

2

The origins of mindfulness

Mindfulness practice and thought is at least 2500 years old.

The story goes that a boy, Siddhartha Gautama, born to a wealthy and powerful family, was brought up in rich seclusion, wanting for nothing. He was kept happy, away from any sights that might have distressed him. When he grew up, he married and had children, all without seeing what lay beyond the walls of the comfortable compound.

One day, curious to know about the world, he escaped from his home to find out more. He soon came face to face with the inevitable hardships of life from which his parents had tried to protect him: suffering, sickness, death and loss.

Overwhelmed by what he saw, he determined to leave his life of riches and find ways to reduce the amount of suffering in the world. He spent many years trying to understand the nature of existence, experimenting with different paths. Eventually, through talking to many sages and wise people, and trying out many distinct practices, he forged his own philosophy and practices.

In particular, Siddhartha Gautama found that by allowing himself to experience 'just being', fully present, in the immediacy of the moment, not grasping to attain any particular feeling or knowledge, he gained deep insights. After meditation, he thought about and debated his insights with others. Mindfulness has its roots in his practices, observations and insights.

Gautama's aim was to reduce suffering through awakening the mind to the way things are:

- That what we experience is largely an interpretation, shaped in our own minds
- That things are impermanent: change is constant
- That if we are always busy chasing after tomorrow, we can fail, constantly, to experience today
- That true happiness comes from a sense of inner peace rather than constantly chasing fleeting emotional 'highs'

~ That mindfulness, or the practice of keeping the mind more 'awakened', can help us to maintain awareness of things that we may 'know', intellectually, but don't usually keep in mind.

When we become more aware, we can recognize how much our own thinking drives us in ways that increase our unhappiness – or create and feed anxiety. We become aware that we can change, and have power over, how we think and act.

Being aware of the inevitability of change

We know, intellectually, that all life is change, in constant flux or impermanence. Signs of this are around us all the time – in the weather, seasons, the passing of traffic, new people being born or entering our lives, relatives and pets getting older, our faces changing in the mirror. Despite this, our minds often act as if things won't change. We cling to habits. We repeat our mistakes. We ignore changes that we don't want to acknowledge. Our thinking, habits and studies get stuck in ruts.

Mindfulness involves recognizing and accepting that all life is change, whether we like that or not. When we are fully aware of this, we can be better at trying to resist the inevitable. Instead, we have the opportunity to really value the current moment, in all its richness.

Change means opportunity to start afresh

Mindfulness involves being aware that we, too, are subject to constant change. We may have been a hero or a villain yesterday, but today we start again. Just because we were a great scholar, or a terrible one, up until this minute, it doesn't mean that will be true, or needs to be true, from now on. If we had bad study habits this morning, we don't need to have them this evening, or ever again.

Studying and study tasks don't last forever either

We act at times as if things we don't like will last forever – as if there will always be an assignment to write, an exam to prepare for, the stress of speaking in front of others in a presentation, the late nights to get the work done. In reality, all of these things last a very short time. Many people look back on their student days with nostalgia, wishing that they had done more with them when they had the chance. Being present in the moment helps us to gain the most from the experience whilst it lasts.

Being aware of time lost to worrying

We can spend a lot of time worrying – in effect, not being present in this moment but concerned about a future condition. Our minds take in what is happening and form a worry; the worry itself comes from our minds. Worrying can arise very easily for most of us. We may even fool ourselves into thinking that we are a better person because of how much we are worrying, or a more committed team member because we are worrying along with everyone else. Worrying doesn't, of itself, achieve anything. It doesn't make things better. It doesn't reduce unhappiness. If we recognize that, and become more aware of the moment when we start to worry, we can think and act differently.

Recognizing signals as helpful friends

Difficult feelings such as pain, anger, fear and shame are useful signals to us that there is something that we need to look at, that we can learn from. When we feel physical pain, we check it, maybe find a cut or bruise and tend to it; our attention can help it heal. Our reaction to psychological pain tends to be different. It is more typical to avoid it, pretending it isn't there or blaming the world, rather than welcoming it as a useful communication. Paying attention to uncomfortable feelings and sensations for a while allows us to become aware of what needs our care and attention.

Meditation can help us

When we meditate, we become aware of many things that elude us when we are racing about our daily lives. We observe the constant rise and fall of the breath, the ebb and flow of sensations, the flurries of thoughts. Once we stop trying to chase after a particular thought, feeling or sensation, we can accept whatever arises just for what it is – the thought that is there that moment which won't be there later. When we focus fully on the present moment, we reduce the mind flitting from thing to thing, cutting out a lot of mental 'noise'. This is calming, and can even lead to feelings of great tranquility and contentment.

The debt to Buddhism

Siddhartha Gautama became known as 'the Buddha', and these philosophies and practices are associated with Buddhism. Drawing on Buddhism doesn't 'make you a Buddhist' – there is a lot more to Buddhist thought and practice.

Buddhism has been, at times, the dominant culture and philosophy in large parts of the world including India, Nepal, Sri Lanka, China, Burma, Korea, Vietnam, Thailand and Indonesia. There are various schools, from Tibetan Buddhism and Japanese Zen to versions adopted in recent centuries in the West. People vary in their views of whether Buddhism is a philosophy, a religion, a culture, a way of life.

You do not need to be religious or a Buddhist to meditate and to take a more mindful approach to life. Indeed, there have been Buddhist traditions, such as those associated with the twentieth-century Burmese teacher Mahasi, that developed such practice for lay people not trained in Buddhist thought. There have been similar movements to bring mindfulness to lay audiences at various points over the last 2000 years. As today, these are not without criticism that a search for a quick fix or rapid results waters down the effects of mindfulness practice, or can divorce the experience from ethics and deeper wisdom (Sharf, 2015).

Mindfulness practice has been spread in the West by a number of teachers, from Nyanaponika Thera in Germany, the Vietnamese teacher Tich Nhat Hanh in France, and Tashi Tsering in the UK, as well as the work of the Dalai Lama around the world, and writers such as Suzuki. This book owes much to them.

Therapies that draw on mindfulness

There are numerous therapies that now combine psychological approaches with aspects of mindfulness practice. Kabat-Zinn's work into Mindfulness-Based Stress Reduction (MBSR) at the University of Massachusetts Medical School led the way. This requires participants to meditate for 45 minutes a day for 8–10 weeks (see pages 22 and 32). Similar approaches have been adopted by various other therapies such as Mindfulness-Based Cognitive Therapy (MBCT).

3

Mindfulness is ...

Mindfulness is ...

- About being fully present in the moment
- Focusing your attention and gently bringing your attention back repeatedly to that focus when it strays
- Being able to 'sit with' whatever arises for you, moment by moment, aware that it will change: it won't stay that way forever
- A pathway to increased awareness, understanding and insight
- A pathway towards greater acceptance of yourself and others.

Mindfulness is achieved through ...

- Intent – wanting to be more self-aware
- Readiness – being open to new experience
- Practice – regular time put aside to develop, observe and direct your attention, such as through simple meditations
- Nurturing feelings of kindness – towards yourself and others
- Observation – noticing what arises, in a focused way
- Reflecting – on your thoughts, actions, feelings, practice
- Application – bringing such focused awareness and insights to everyday life, including study if that is what you are engaged in.

Mindfulness practice can be used to ...

- Develop greater attention, concentration and focus
- Enhance learning and study
- Cultivate empathy and understanding
- Foster self-awareness and personal development
- Experience calm
- Improve sleep, health and well-being
- Manage anxiety, pain and unhelpful stress levels
- Cope better with difficult and challenging situations.

Seven facets of mindfulness

1) **A mental state of enhanced awareness**

Mindfulness is primarily about enhanced consciousness or 'awareness'. You can think of it as a mind 'awakened' to see things more clearly and accurately.

2) **An intention to be more aware**

You can't force mindfulness, awareness, or the benefits of these. You start with an intent to be more mindful, and then take actions that nurture it.

3) **An experience**

If you maintain your practice, it is likely that there will be times when you experience things differently, or think about your experience differently.

4) **A way of thinking**

Mindfulness brings awareness of the power of our own minds to interpret and shape our experience and the world around us. Although we may 'know' this, intellectually, mindfulness meditations bring deeper levels of clarity and insight into our typical thought patterns and how these affect us.

5) **A way of behaving and being**

You can apply mindfulness to everyday life and work, including study, so that you act in a more considered way. In effect, you become more aware of the relationship between thought, action and consequence.

6) **A useful tool**

Mindfulness is gaining recognition as a tool for managing difficult and stressful situations.

7) **An ability**

Mindfulness becomes an ability to direct your attention more effectively, enabling you to better manage emotions, thoughts, actions and situations. The more you practise, the more skilled you become at changing your mood, attitude and responses as soon as these arise.

Mindfulness as development

An 'awakened' mind that can see things clearly and is able to direct those insights to good effect.

A developing ability to move into states of greater awareness, and to manage your level of awareness.

A way of being and living Your insights help you understand the importance of awareness and compassion; this, in turn, can prompt you to call upon mindfulness as part of your everyday thinking.

A growing understanding of the more subtle and nuanced ways that your thoughts, actions, feelings and consequences are connected.

An experience The practice of mindfulness can produce a different sense of your experience, either in the moment or in general.

An enhanced awareness of your own thoughts and the power these have over your attitudes, actions, feelings, life.

Mindfulness ...

Affects how you feel, think, behave, learn ...

Leading to ever more mindful thoughts and actions ...

Influencing the content of your brain and thoughts, as well as how you think (your thinking processes) ...

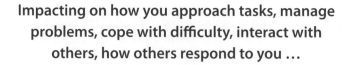

Enabling greater focus, attention, concentration, learning, contentment, calm, health, well-being ...

Impacting on how you approach tasks, manage problems, cope with difficulty, interact with others, how others respond to you ...

Shaping how you perceive the world, your place in it, the value of your actions, the value of others, and the relative significance of what you experience within the 'bigger picture'.

4

Why mindfulness?

Because of all of those distractions ...

~ Because we are bombarded with stimuli, especially from our devices, TV, social media

~ Because there are many demands on us, which can make it difficult to 'switch off'

~ Because everyday life can be exhausting, excessively stressful and overwhelming.

Because of how we respond to distractions ...

~ Because we get distracted from what is important or from things we need to do

~ Because we think we can multi-task and divide our attention – and deceive ourselves into thinking we manage this well

~ Because we use distraction to prevent ourselves from having to deal with emotions and truths about ourselves that we find uncomfortable.

Because we don't always know ourselves well ...

~ Because we are good at deluding ourselves, believing what we want to believe

~ Because our thoughts and feelings can seem to rule us, rather than the other way around

~ Because we don't make time to sit alone quietly and take notice

~ Because we don't put time aside to notice what we are really thinking, feeling, doing, and the consequences of these.

Because it can induce calm ...

~ Mindfulness practice creates a sense of being 'centred'

~ The stillness associated with practice can be calming

~ The concepts associated with mindfulness provide a way of thinking that helps in managing difficult thoughts and situations.

Why mindfulness for students?

Because it can be hard to get down to study ...

~ Because we are good at finding ways of putting it off until later

~ Because we don't clarify, sufficiently, what is expected

~ Because we want to do other things instead

~ Because we decide we are bored, can't do it, or it is too easy.

Because attention can drift when studying

~ Because we can get to the end of a page and not remember a word of what we have read

~ Because we can take lots of notes in a lecture, without thinking about the information or absorbing it

~ Because we can read the instructions on an exam paper and not take these in, leading to mistakes

~ Because we waste time through inefficient study habits arising from poor concentration and self-awareness.

Because we can bring unhelpful attitudes to study

- Because we let our focus on grades and results get out of balance
- Because we can bring too little awareness to the process of learning and to understanding our subjects
- Because we don't always appreciate the benefits of mental challenge and stretching our minds
- Because we might 'switch off' when learning is difficult rather than sticking with it or changing gear.

Because student life can be over-stimulating

- There are so many demands on time
- It is easy to get distracted by social media and the internet

- There are so many new people to meet
- There are so many different kinds of opportunities to choose between or juggle
- It involves lots of new knowledge and ideas that can leave the mind racing
- It can be easy to lose a sense of calm and focus.

Because student life can feel difficult

What if I don't pass? Will I ever get a good job?

~ It is a big investment of time and money so there can be pressure to succeed

~ Because study is designed to stretch us intellectually, and sometimes that feels too much

~ Because assignments, exams and classes can seem too hard

~ Because waiting for grades and exam results can be nerve-wracking

~ Because it can be hard to receive feedback and critiques, even when these could help us.

Because of all the focus on the future

~ On taking notes for future reference

~ On planning for the future

~ On forthcoming deadlines and exams

~ On making choices about next year's study

~ On gaining a graduate job and career

~ On future success, maybe as defined by other people.

… All of which have a place, but which can distract and detract from enjoyment of study in the moment.

🧘 Reflection: Personal interest in mindfulness

~ Why are you interested in mindfulness?

~ What are your initial thoughts about how it might help you?

5

What does mindfulness involve?

What would I have to do?

- Be open to the experience and commit to giving it a go.
- Learn some basic techniques, such as simple meditations.
- Practise these, ideally for a short period at least once a day.
- Reflect on what arises for you, drawing on certain concepts that provide a way of thinking about your experience.
- Call upon the techniques, concepts and your insights in everyday life, as and when that feels useful.

Is it difficult?

You can think about this in terms of techniques, practice, application and outcomes.

The basic techniques can be learnt quickly. There is guidance provided in Part 2 and there are many websites, books and recordings that you can choose from if you wish to draw on alternative wording. You can keep mindfulness as simple as you wish – simplicity helps.

Establishing a daily meditation practice is easy for some people, less so for others. It is less easy if it feels it is competing with other things. You can expect days (maybe even every day!) when you won't feel like practising or it seems hard to find the time. It is entirely up to you whether you do so. It is easier if you create dedicated time and space, so it feels as though it occupies a natural place in your day. It is also easier once you have found some enjoyment in the process – and many people enjoy both meditation and its after-effects.

It can be a challenge to remember to apply mindfulness during everyday life and study, where it can do most good. Like most skills and habits, it gets easier the more you do it.

As with many things that are simple, maintaining a mindful state of being is not at all easy. It is important not to become too attached to being perfectly mindful all the time or to perceived potential outcomes. Allow yourself to enjoy the process and let the benefits arise without being forced.

What are the benefits?

Mindfulness uses quite simple techniques such as bringing your awareness gently to your breath. In the short term, this can generate feelings of calm. Longer term, this can develop a range of attributes, including improved concentration, thinking skills, problem-solving and people skills. It can also improve health and well-being. For more details, see Chapter 8.

Who can benefit from mindfulness?

Anyone can learn to be more mindful and improve attention, focus and attitude. You just need to be open to it and practise.

If you are receiving medical support for mental ill health, or have concerns about depression or anxiety, it is a good idea to talk this through with your doctor, medical adviser or counsellor first. Give thought to whether to start mindfulness practice at this time, especially if meditating alone.

You may benefit from starting to meditate with a group: your university or college support services should be able to suggest a local group or class.

How long does it take to feel benefits?

You can feel some immediate benefit from even a few moments of mindful attention to the breath. That can be useful for managing everyday situations. For longer-term effects, some people find that they start to feel calmer or more focused after a few days or weeks. In therapeutic and research contexts which have identified beneficial changes, it is typical to use at least eight-week periods of daily meditation and weekly or daily classes (see pages 12 and 32).

The effects can be profound and life changing, especially for people who maintain a regular practice over the longer term.

What do I need to get started?

~ You can practise mindfulness anywhere, any time, without any special equipment or furniture.

~ It is useful to keep a journal to reflect on your experience. This can be in any format or size that suits you, paper-based or electronic.

~ For beginners, it is useful to have a quiet space where you will not be interrupted for at least a few minutes every day.

~ For some meditations, you will need a few other items (see page 46).

What is the time commitment?

It is up to you. There are no rules. For set exercises and meditations, you can start with a few minutes (see page 47). The more you think about mindfulness, the more it becomes just a part of the way you approach life. The following are recommended.

1. 10–45 minutes, once or twice a day, of mindfulness exercises and meditation – known as your 'practice'.

2. A few moments here and there during the day recalling the experience or insights of mindfulness practice and applying them to a task you are undertaking.

3. A few minutes every few days or so to jot down observations and reflections, or to read back over these and think about them.

Intention

- **An intent** to bring conscious awareness to your experience as it unfolds moment by moment, without judging it.

- **Willingness** to give it a go and openness to its potential benefits.

- **Commitment** to developing mindfulness as a habit, putting time aside for this purpose.

Feelings

- **Kindness and compassion towards yourself**, including generating and nurturing feelings of self-awareness and self-compassion.

- **Compassion and empathy for others**, including generating and nurturing feelings of kindness, understanding and empathy for others.

Action

- **Meditation**, to nurture a more aware and compassionate mind.

- **Practice** undertaken regularly and frequently.

- **Applying insights** to whatever situations you find yourself in, such as your study, decision-making, work, everyday life.

- **Practical action** – bringing an enhanced awareness to bear on your everyday thoughts, actions, behaviours and feelings.

Awareness

- Enhanced self-awareness.

- Enhanced awareness of why mindfulness is important.

- Enhanced awareness of the power of the mind to effect changes in thought patterns, attitudes, feelings, emotions, behaviours, events and outcomes.

6

Why meditation and where does it fit in?

What is meditation?

Meditation is a means of training the mind to be more aware of itself. Over time, practitioners become better not only at becoming conscious of the contents of their minds at a given moment, but also at noticing such things as the moment when their attention is starting to wander, and the effects of their thoughts on their emotional and physical reactions. Regular practice, along with observation and reflection, helps the transfer of such mental skills into everyday life. This can lead to the formation of good habits for managing difficult situations, improving well-being and developing empathy for the self and others.

The word 'meditation' derives from the Latin 'meditari', meaning to 'think about' or contemplate. There are many forms of meditation practice. These recommend diverse techniques for developing positive attributes such as calm, energy, generosity, patience and compassion, depending on the traditions from which they emerge. Many religions from Hinduism to Judaism, Christianity, Islam and Bahá'i have meditative traditions, although meditation techniques do not necessarily have a religious component and are used in secular therapeutic and workplace contexts.

Mindfulness meditation

In the context of mindfulness, meditation means:

1. Directing all your attention to the object of your focus (the breath, an action, an object, etc.).

2. Noticing when your attention drifts onto something else.

3. Without judging, simply bringing your attention back to the intended focus, letting go of judgements, emotions, thoughts, annoyance.

4. And then starting again. And again. Appreciating the opportunity that comes from starting again.

If you are new to meditation, don't be put off by the term. It is not complicated and step-by-step guidance, tips and FAQs are provided.

Do I have to meditate to be mindful?

You can be mindful without meditation, in the sense of bringing a thoughtful and/or compassionate response to what you are doing. We use expressions associated with 'mindfulness' in everyday language to remind us to be 'aware', 'pay attention', 'remember' or 'take care':

~ *Mind the gap – in case you fall over the edge of the platform when getting off the train*

~ *I am mindful that this is a sensitive issue for them*

~ *I am aware of how important it is to make a good impression when I meet my professor/prospective employer/etc.*

~ *Take care how you go today: it is icy outside*

~ *I am conscious of the time and that I need to finish by 5 p.m.*

In such moments, we aim to be more aware than usual of what we are thinking, doing, saying, feeling.

Mindfulness meditation trains and develops your mind so that you are better able to catch and manage your response to whatever you experience – your thoughts, actions, moods and emotions. It provides:

~ the mental space to train your mind

~ time-honoured methods for doing so

~ a useful and accessible focus.

What is meditation like?

You will probably find that each meditation session is different. Some sessions will feel great, others frustrating. Some may surprise you by the impact on your state of well-being, happiness and consciousness. Some may not feel like anything in particular.

You may find that there are weeks when you focus easily, and others where your attention just drifts a lot. That is normal. It is important to recognize that and just keep going. Changing your posture, the time of day, or what you do before meditation may help shift a change in the experience.

What happens in the brain when you meditate?

Scientists at the Flinders Medical Centre for Neuroscience found that during meditation, there is an increase in alpha brainwaves; these are associated with being focused and paying attention. Delta brainwaves, linked to feeling sleepy, decrease in meditative states, suggesting heightened alertness (Sydney Morning Herald, 2007).

During meditation itself, we reduce the amount of things on which the brain needs to focus, so it processes less information. Research at Harvard University using Magnetic Resonance Imaging (MRI) found that mindfulness meditation decreases beta wave activity. Beta waves indicate when the brain is processing information. Hölzel et al. (2011) used MRI to identify those parts of the brain where beta waves decreased the most during meditation. They found:

~ Very little beta activity in the frontal lobe, the part of the brain responsible for reasoning, emotions and self-conscious awareness

~ Slower activity in the parietal lobe, responsible for using sensory information from the environment to orientate us in time and space

~ Little incoming activity in the thalamus, which acts as a 'gatekeeper' for sending, or withholding, sensory data to the rest of the brain.

Changes to parts of brain associated with intelligence

Over time, whatever we use our brain for affects the structure of the brain. If we spend more time in juggling, driving taxis, meditating or being anxious, this affects the neural structures of the brain, showing up in the amount of grey matter in the parts of the brain associated with that activity.

Meditation increases the amount of grey matter in those regions of the brain associated with intelligence, memory, language, and learning. Cortical thickness is correlated with intelligence and in selected regions, this has been found to get thicker the more time (in years) that people meditate. On the other hand, grey matter decreases in the amygdala, the part of the brain associated with stress and anxiety, suggesting that meditators spend less time stressed (Lazar et al., 2005; Holzel et al., 2011; Narr et al., 2007).

What do I need for meditations?

It is possible to meditate anywhere – in your room, on the bus or train, whilst walking, washing the dishes, etc. However, if you are seated for more than a few minutes for mindfulness exercises and meditations, the following items are recommended.

- a chair where you can sit upright comfortably – or some firm cushions to support you sitting on the floor
- a cushion on which to rest your hands
- a timer, to let you know when your meditation time is up
- a place where you won't be disturbed whilst practising
- a journal to reflect on your experience.

Some people like to use candles to create a calm environment before starting to meditate and for sitting quietly for a while afterwards to collect their thoughts. You can opt to use a meditation bell or bowl to commence a meditation and then to bring meditation to an end.

How much time does it take?

To get started, it is best to begin with just a few minutes, and gradually build these to 20–45 minutes. Some people like to practise for longer. However, you can call upon meditation techniques in everyday life, even for just a few seconds, to help you cope with challenging situations.

Must I spend the same amount of time every day?

That isn't necessary. It is better to practise regularly for a short time rather than set high demands on your time that prevent regular practice. That said, many people do find it easier to keep going if they put aside the same time every day. It builds a useful habit and sense of routine.

How long do I need to stick with the practice?

Experienced practitioners continue to practise across their lifetime – it is really up to you how long you decide to practise.

What if I stopped practising for a while?

It is not unusual for people to drift from practice, then return to it. It is easy to start again whenever you want.

7

What can I expect?

If you are new to mindfulness, and especially to meditation, you may be wondering what to expect. It is very distinct for each person, and from one day to the next. The following comments from both beginners and more experienced meditators provide an idea of the kinds of experiences you might expect.

Typical reactions for beginners

I liked the breathing exercises. I feel they are doing me good.

I struggled hard against drifting off. I have a lot on my mind.

It was amazing. I felt like I was filled with happiness.

I felt really sleepy – I found it hard not to nod off.

It was good actually. I don't know if it is the meditation and talking about it, but I do feel we get on better as a team since we started this together. More considerate.

I can concentrate better when I'm reading and writing in my room if I do a short meditation first.

For me, walking meditation is more natural. I do five minutes every now and again during the day to get a break from my desk. My concentration is better afterwards.

I think I am trying too hard to 'do it right'. I feel frustrated but I am determined not to give up yet.

I didn't feel anything in particular – I liked the quiet, the calm.

And from those meditating for 10 years or more ...

I really enjoy sitting quietly. I used to think it was important to do, but didn't have a sense of what a treat it would be – a gift really ... It helps me manage life, my feelings, not being overwhelmed, being more aware of the world around me, of what matters to me.

Some days are good, some days are amazing, really joyful, some days it does just feel like 'practising'! Before I start, I never know how it will turn out, although I have got much better at setting up my meditation so that it is likely to be focused, more comfortable, even more enjoyable.

Everything is useful in the long run. It all feeds in somewhere. You just can't always see it for a while.

If I have a lot in my mind, or haven't set up my meditation well, I still struggle. Maybe I can't find a comfortable position and I'm fidgeting; I want to stop and do something else. I used to give up at that point. Then one day, I realized that sitting with myself meant sitting with my 'fidgety' self too. I find now that if I stay still, just following my breath, I stop fidgeting after a while, and become more tranquil.

After 20 years, I feel I am still a beginner!

Meditation can be unpredictable ...

Some days it is very easy to get into meditation and you will decide to continue to sit and enjoy it for longer.

Occasionally, you may feel full of unexpected joy, that your body and mind are aligned and in tune, a sense of deep contentment and tranquility, that you are alert, calm, joyful, serene, kind and empathetic.

Often, you can't get comfortable, don't feel like meditating, can't focus – and then you realize that working with this is what sharpens your mind.

At times, you become aware of sadness, anger, anxiety, grief or other deep emotions. Observing these emotions in meditation helps you to realize, or maybe remember, that it is possible for you to experience such feelings without being overwhelmed by them. You are more than your emotions. You can carry this awareness into other situations where you need to manage big feelings and emotions.

Stick with it ...

For most people, the experience appears to be beneficial. According to many surveys that ask participants to self-report on the effects of mindfulness meditation, there is some positive result even for beginners. However, it isn't helpful to expect instant results. You reap the benefits through practising over the longer term, and by focusing on your practice, rather than trying to force any particular experience.

8

Evidence of the benefits

Research indicates that meditation leads to both short-term and long-term benefits across a very wide range of circumstances. Over time, continued mindfulness practice can even change the brain, structurally and chemically, in beneficial ways. Research into this area is still relatively new, so it is likely that further research may modify or reinforce these early indications.

However, although research methodologies are improving and refining our understanding of how and why mindfulness is effective, the huge body of research studies indicates that mindfulness practice is worthwhile. The benefits include such things as:

~ Improved mental concentration

~ Improved memory and recall

~ Improved performance and better grades for students

~ Strengthening of the immune system against colds, flu and other ailments

~ Reduced anxiety, stress and depression

~ Improved emotional self-management

~ Increased empathy and improved interpersonal skills

~ Increased contentment and sense of well-being.

The reported benefits to performance, efficient thinking, interpersonal relationships and well-being are so wide-ranging that it is not surprising that businesses, large and small, are investing in mindfulness training for their employees. These include the US Army, Google, Whitehall, and many others (Good et al., 2015). NICE (National Institute for Health and Care Excellence) in the UK recognizes the value of mindfulness for addressing psychological stress.

Some key research findings are indicated below. Studies into the benefits to students are considered in Chapter 9 (pages 34–5) and in the chapters related to specific study tasks.

What does research tell us about how mindfulness makes a difference?

Academic and work performance There is a great deal of research that indicates that mindfulness improves abilities associated with good performance, such as attention and concentration. Continued practice changes the structure of the brain, helping to cement this advantage. It has been found that practised meditators have thicker cortical regions of the brain: these regions are associated with attention and intelligence (Lazar et al., 2005). See page 27.

Empathy Metta-style meditation (Chapter 21) increases neural activation in parts of the brain that pick up on emotional cues. This suggests a capacity for greater empathy and interpersonal skills (Lutz et al., 2008).

Creativity and 'whole person' development A report on the findings of over 40 years of research found that, as well as cognitive benefits, mindfulness practice enhanced a wide range of abilities and personal attributes, from increased creativity and self-compassion to empathy and interpersonal skills (Shapiro et al., 2008).

Reducing negative impacts from other people's emotions Studies with nursing professionals have found that mindfulness not only increased their empathy, but also reduced the likelihood of their absorbing other people's negative emotions (Beddoe and Murphy, 2004; Shapiro et al., 2005).

Improved health and immune system Research indicates that the immune system's antibody production can be boosted even after 8 weeks of meditation. This has obvious benefits for resisting disease.

Depression and stress Mindfulness Based Cognitive Therapy (MBCT) has been used with people experiencing depression, providing training in observing their thoughts and feelings without self-judgement (see page 12). Those taking MBCT courses are less likely to relapse into depression: 37% compared with 66% for those who didn't undertake the course (Teasdale et al., 2000).

9

How mindfulness can benefit students

Managing the challenges of higher-level study

Higher-level study, whilst offering a fantastic opportunity to learn and grow as a person, is also a challenge. It is meant to stretch you intellectually. It encourages you to grapple with difficult concepts and problems, and to deal with issues for which there are no clear and easy answers. That can be exciting, and you gain from the intellectual stretch, but sometimes it can feel too much.

In addition, it is likely that you are grappling with other demands outside of study, such as juggling work, family and other important commitments. You may be away from home for the first time, missing family, friends, all that is familiar to you. You may be managing your time, motivation or money for the first time, or grappling with new life and social skills. All of these circumstances can create unhelpful levels of distraction, stress and anxiety. Mindfulness can help.

Managing emotions and anxiety

Mindfulness practice has been shown to improve general well-being and abilities in managing situations that create high levels of stress. This means it is useful for helping students to cope better with stressful times, such as settling into study or a new group, the lead-up to exams, giving presentations or going for work placement interviews. For more on using mindfulness to alleviate stress, see Chapter 46.

However, although there has been much emphasis in recent decades on the benefits of mindfulness practice for mental well-being, mindfulness is not primarily about stress management. It offers a lot more, including benefits for study.

What does research tell us about how mindfulness assists study?

A great deal of research has been undertaken into how mindfulness benefits different aspects of study; this will be introduced in the relevant chapters in Part 3. At this point, it is worth noting just some ways that research indicates that mindfulness practice can benefit study. Consider these, identifying ☑ those that are relevant to you.

☐ **Better grades and intellectual performance**
Mindfulness practice has been associated with brain changes, abilities and behaviours associated with improved intellectual performance (Good et al., 2015; Smallwood and Schooler, 2015). In one study with college students by Hall (1999), students who meditated for 10 minutes at the start and end of a one-hour study group twice a week, as well as being instructed to meditate before exams, achieved much better grades than a control group of students. The control group had had similar grades at the start of the year but wasn't trained to meditate.

☐ **Better memory and recall**
Mindfulness practice is associated with greater capacity in working memory (Roeser et al., 2013). This is useful for all aspects of study. Good recall means we can draw on our knowledge easily in order to apply it to new situations, such as in class, on work placement, in professional life, as well as for tests and exams.

☐ **Improved ability in making sense of new information**
Research indicates that mindfulness meditation helps us to process and respond to new information through greater abilities in assessing patterns and relationships (Tang et al., 2007; Gard et al., 2014). This benefits students, as manipulating new information, and seeing trends and connections, are core to learning and to developing understanding.

☐ **Flexible thinking**
Mindfulness develops abilities in generating new ways of looking at things and responding to new situations (Walsh, 1995). This benefits students in further and higher education, where there is a premium on thinking in innovative ways and being open to challenging concepts.

☐ **Creative thinking and problem-solving abilities**

These skills are indicated in research by Ostafin and Kassman (2012) and Ding et al. (2015). They benefit students on most programmes, not just those on creative courses. Most courses set intellectual challenges that require students to think creatively and generate their own solutions.

☐ **Greater awareness**

Mindfulness practice promotes awareness. As a student, you will find this can bring greater recognition of thought patterns and behaviours that may be getting in the way of your studies. Greater self-awareness feeds into many aspects of study and student life, such as motivation, decision-making, and the development of good study habits, all of which can improve your learning experience and support your success.

☐ **Improved attention, concentration and focus**

Although we can learn in unconscious ways, much of the time the mental processes involved in learning are dependent on attention (LaBerge, 1995). Attention, concentration and focus are useful attributes to develop, to benefit almost any aspect of study, and especially for complex issues that require sustained investigation, reading and thought. They are of value whether you are studying independently in the library, following a discussion in class, or trying to stay alert during long lectures or seminars. This is examined further in Chapters 37–9 on the effects of task-switching and multi-tasking.

☐ **A focus on method rather than an end point**

We can spend a great deal of time thinking about what we would like to achieve, academically or otherwise, rather than just focusing fully on what we are doing and doing it well. Mindfulness practice doesn't mean we need to abandon our goals but, rather, draws our awareness to the process of getting there, as experienced in the moment. You take more notice of the actions you are engaged in along the way. If you do those well, you gain satisfaction from the process of studying, irrespective of what grades you attain. Whether or not you achieve your original goal – you have a better experience, you learn more, and you understand more about yourself.

☐ **'Stick-with-it-ness'**
It usually takes several years to gain a qualification. This calls for a high level of perseverance. In that time, it is easy to lose motivation and focus. Mindfulness practice develops the ability to stick with a task, and to keep returning to it, even when there might be no perceptible immediate reward. It trains you to stay on task, and to appreciate the value of doing so.

☐ **Development of empathy**
Mindfulness, or maintaining full awareness in the moment, is almost impossible to achieve for any length of time, despite being simple. The constant loss of attention during meditation, despite your good intent, can bring a certain humility that helps you to empathize when others find apparently simple things difficult.

Mindfulness practice trains you to experience without blaming and judging yourself for lapses in attention. This can be harder than expected, as the act of constantly returning to the breath can lead to rapid self-judgement. Alongside mindfulness practice, it is traditional to practise a meditation in kindness towards yourself and others (Chapter 21). Combined, these meditations can be powerful in developing self-compassion and empathy towards others. Such qualities are beneficial in a range of contexts, from coping with stressful situations through to social learning, group work, collaborative projects, supporting others, and working or learning with many different kinds of people.

♠ Reflection: Relevance to me of mindfulness's benefits

~ Which of these benefits are the most relevant to you?
~ Are there any of these benefits that you consider are not relevant to you?

10

Are there any risks or downsides?

Assuming mindfulness is a 'magic solution'

When you read about the long list of benefits associated with mindfulness practice, it can sound like a magical pill. A few minutes of focusing on the breath and all your problems will disappear! Of course, it isn't like that in reality. On the other hand, it isn't helpful to dismiss the benefits of mindfulness practice on the basis that its effects are hard to measure numerically and under artificially contrived conditions.

The efficacy of mindfulness practice should be considered in the context of individuals or groups, their situation and their practice. Ultimately, for you, it is your practice and experience that should count.

A 'quick fix'?

Research undertaken into the success of mindfulness practice, or into therapies that make use of it, indicates that even a little mindfulness training can be beneficial. Whilst some people do seem to experience rapid change, it isn't helpful to expect instant, long-lasting results. It is reasonable to assume there may be some, but limited, effects …

- ~ if you have had only a short exposure to mindfulness training
- ~ if you do not have an established daily meditation practice, or at least regular and frequent practice
- ~ if you don't maintain that meditation practice.

It is useful to remember that 'mindfulness' has traditionally involved daily meditation and conscious effort to bring awareness into everyday experiences. This was expected to be a way of life, lasting a lifetime, rather than a transient means of addressing specific problems.

It brings constant and varied challenges

The experience of mindfulness is very varied, not just from one person to another, but for every individual. Even within a single sitting, you may find that you go through distinct periods of happiness, contentment, day-dreaming, frustration, impatience, discomfort, anger, sadness and so on. Sometimes you can't shake off those feelings, and they stay with you during the meditation and possibly afterwards too.

Over time, you can come to recognize that this is all useful: the range of experience in meditation is essential in order to work with a variety of experiences outside of it, with the full gamut of thoughts and feelings. This variety, however uncomfortable, builds your neural response (the way your brain is structured), enabling different cognitive and emotional responses: you have more conscious control over how you think and feel. Continued mindfulness makes it easier to achieve a balanced response in the face of whatever challenges life throws at you.

Becoming aware of difficult thoughts and emotions

Through mindfulness practice, you train yourself to be 'fully present' in the moment, more aware of whatever is present. At some point, it is likely that you will come face to face with memories and thoughts that make you unhappy, anxious, rageful and agitated. You may feel shame at ways that you have behaved, or realize that particular thought patterns don't serve you well any more. If you are aware that this can happen, at least you are a little prepared, and it will come as less of a shock.

Self-criticism

One consequence of mindfulness practice is that, at some stage, you are likely to recognize that some aspects of the way you lead your life are not beneficial to you or perhaps to others. Sometimes, that can be difficult to face. It is easy to fall into self-criticism and to drift away from practice at that point. If you feel like this, it is useful to:

- talk to a mindfulness trainer or experienced practitioner, or to a counsellor who has experience of mindfulness practice
- alternate mindfulness meditations with those that focus on kindness, or stay with kindness meditations for a while (see Chapter 21).

It can require strength of character

Sometimes, it takes a great deal of courage and a strong will:

- to sit with intense feelings and uncomfortable thoughts, bringing your attention back to the breath, over and over again
- to return to meditation when you have had a difficult session or have drifted away from practising
- to prioritize regular mindfulness practice and stick with it through good times and bad
- to find time for mindfulness practice with all the work, study, opportunities and distractions that make demands on students' time and energies.

When you persevere with your practice under such conditions, you develop strong personal qualities that help you for study and in a wide variety of other life situations.

Experiencing difficult thoughts and emotions?

It is likely that at some time, you will find that your practice will seem hard. If so, you have choices. For example, you can:

- Notice what you are feeling and bring your attention back to your breath – repeatedly, if necessary. A few minutes of focused breathing can have a dramatic effect, leaving you feeling much better. However, it may not always have that effect.
- Imagine the blue sky filling your mind – see page 101.
- Remind yourself that your emotional response to painful memories is being generated by your mind, and that your mind can cease to dwell on them, at least for now.
- Change to a 'Metta' meditation (page 73), and focus just on yourself or others who are relevant to the feelings you are having.
- Stop the meditation if the feelings are too painful. You don't have to persist. Take a few minutes to yourself.
- Write your thoughts down in a journal.
- Speak to friends, family, a meditation class leader, or a student counsellor.

For those with severe anxiety and mental ill-health

If you experience severe anxiety, depression or other mental health conditions, mindfulness can be really helpful if managed correctly, but it can also be very challenging. If you practise mindfulness meditations, you might be all the more aware of the things that you find problematic already, and you may become aware of difficult thoughts and emotions that you were not conscious of previously.

For these reasons, it is strongly advisable to take some steps before engaging in mindfulness, and certainly before developing a daily practice. These are:

1. Talk it over first with your medical advisers and/or therapist. Let them know what you decide, and listen to their advice.

2. Find a mindfulness teacher or trainer who has been training for a number of years. Ideally, find one who has experience of people with similar conditions or experiences to your own.

3. Make sure you have some kind of social network around you so that you have other things to do rather than just dwell on what comes up in meditation.

4. Join a meditation class or group at a local centre or a group set up specifically for people with your mental health concerns.

5. If possible, bring a friend with you to the training. It will reduce some of your surrounding anxieties about being in a new place, with new people, trying out something you haven't yet experienced. Let them know that if you want to leave early, you would like them to leave with you.

6. Sit near the door so that you can leave quietly and easily if you need to. It is usually very quiet in meditation groups so it may feel daunting to get up to leave. However, it doesn't matter if you do or if you make a noise. Alternatively, you can just sit quietly and wait until everyone has finished.

11

Myths and misconceptions about mindfulness

The solution to all problems?

Mindfulness practice can lead to a wide range of benefits and positive outcomes but it isn't an instant remedy for all ills. It can't solve all your problems, although it can help you to cope with them better and to feel better in doing so. See Chapter 10.

'You have to set goals for mindfulness to work'

Mindfulness meditation is more likely to work if you don't push for goals or outcomes – it needs a 'non-grasping' mind. It is better to be open to possibilities, reflect on them and on your practice, and let the process work rather than trying to force it to deliver particular goals.

'You notice changes straight away'

Research indicates that there is an impact on brain and biology after just a little mindfulness meditation, even if you don't notice it. You may experience changes immediately but that is not necessarily the case. Some people do; some do not. Either way, the effects are likely to be subtle, possibly hard to notice for a while. These build over time, so you might not notice a sudden change.

You have to 'empty your mind' of all thoughts

It is often assumed that mindfulness means you have to 'clear your mind of thoughts' or 'stop thinking'. As a result of this misconception, when people start meditating and find that thoughts keep coming, they think they can't do it, and so they stop. The mind is constantly filling with thoughts. In mindfulness, you become more aware of what these are, and train your mind to better manage your mental and physical responses to these. It is likely that you will learn to reduce mental 'noise', but thoughts will still arise.

'You must have a calm place to practise'

Having calm surroundings can be useful, but is not essential. You can even welcome occasional noises for bringing your awareness back from day-dreaming (see page 68). Over time, you can learn to draw on your mindfulness practice to help you maintain inner calm whatever the outer circumstances.

If you prefer to meditate in a quiet place, that is fine. It can help to:

- ~ Put up a 'Do not disturb' sign on your door when meditating
- ~ Join a group that has a regular room booked
- ~ Use college 'chaplaincy' services
- ~ Ask at student services where you might find a quiet space on campus.

'My mind is just too fast to meditate'

If you have the kind of mind that races with thoughts and ideas, it is likely that you need mindfulness all the more. You may need more practice but you are likely to feel the benefits more strongly too. Stick with it.

Part 2

Techniques

12

Introducing the techniques

About the techniques

The techniques outlined in this section are routes or pathways to developing mindfulness. They are not the same as 'mindfulness' itself, which is a state of mind. That mental state can arise during practice or outside of it. Ideally, through continued practice, observation, reflection, thoughtfulness and application, such a mental state becomes a habit. It can infuse the way you live your life, the way you go about studying, learning, living, being in the world.

Where to start in learning these techniques

1. Starter exercises

~ Begin with the Starter Exercises (pages 47–60), reading the preparation notes for these first (page 46).

2. Core meditations

~ Then learn Mindfulness of Breathing (page 62).

~ Practise four-stage Mindfulness of Breathing (pages 63–4).

~ Learn the Metta meditation (mindful kindness; page 74).

~ Set up a daily practice, alternating Mindfulness of Breathing with Metta.

3. Additional exercises and practices

~ Look for opportunities to bring a mindful awareness and attitude into your everyday life and study. You can do so at any time for as long or short a time as you choose.

~ Have a go at applying mindfulness to various everyday activities, such as walking, travelling and eating. See pages 87–96.

Preparation

Making time: Put time aside for these exercises and respect it as 'time apart' from the everyday rush.

Keeping track of time: Set a clock or timer to signal when the time for the exercise or meditation is up. This means you don't need to be distracted by watching the clock.

Location: Ideally, find a quiet space where you won't be disturbed. However, any space can be fine.

Distractions: Remove distractions, turn off devices and ensure you won't be interrupted.

Seating: For seated exercises, use a comfortable seat where you can sit upright and comfortably, with your back supported and your feet flat on the floor. If you prefer, sit cross-legged on the floor on a couple of firm cushions. See also the section on posture, page 82.

Resting your hands: Rest your hands in your lap, on your thighs, or on a cushion. You may prefer to use a folded towel or jumper.

Eyes open or closed? Unless the exercise specifies keeping eyes open or closed, then it is up to you. Closing your eyes can be useful for maintaining your focus. If you prefer to keep your eyes open, focus your attention on a point below and in front of you.

'Tools': People often find it helpful to light a candle and watch the flame before they begin or end an exercise. Incense can also help to establish a sense of time and place, which helps the mind prepare for meditation. Traditionally, meditators struck a metal bowl or rang a bell and let their attention follow the diminishing sound to start off their meditation; sounding firmer notes at the end of the time brought the attention out of meditation. These can be useful for setting up a routine that prepares your mind for the exercise or meditation, but they are not essential.

13

Starter exercises

These exercises provide a gentle introduction to mindfulness and ease you into meditation. Return to them at any time to assist your practice. Ideally, use each at least twice, spending a few minutes each time.

Read the preparation notes and exercise guidance notes each time to get the gist of what to do. Don't worry about getting exercises exactly right – through practice you will come to remember what to do.

1. Just noticing (pages 49–50)

Mindfulness is about greater awareness, so focusing the attention is a good starting place. This is a good calming exercise and a mental 'warm-up' for mindfulness meditations.

2. Seeing an object – with new eyes (pages 51–2)

This exercise is useful for developing calm and concentration. It is a good reminder to us of how what we see changes if we really observe.

3. Appreciation of stillness (pages 53–6)

Our daily lives don't often allow us to appreciate the value of stillness and silence. It might even feel odd or disquieting at first. Just being with yourself, quietly, can be powerful, not least in getting to know yourself and experience calm. If you can appreciate stillness and silence for their own sakes, then it is easier to value and enjoy time spent in meditation.

4. Awareness of body and breath (pages 57–60)

It can be tempting to rush into mindfulness meditations without taking stock of how we feel mentally and physically. Practising this exercise helps to establish good meditation habits from the start. Observing your physical state is useful generally, such as being aware of your posture for reading or when using computer screens and portable devices.

14

'Just noticing'

This is a good warm-up for any session of mindfulness. All you need to do is sit still, listen, notice. You don't have to 'achieve' anything.

Guidance

Time: 5 Minutes

- Read through the preparation notes on page 46.
- Close your eyes. Smile gently to loosen your facial muscles. Then let your face relax.
- Notice what it feels like to be sitting still, doing nothing.
- Bring your awareness to any sounds in the room or outside. Don't describe them – just notice them. You may notice such things as your tummy rumbling; cars approaching, passing, and moving away; voices outside, loud or quiet; the heating systems, air conditioning, floorboards or furniture creaking; footsteps passing; a door closing; birdsong; dogs barking; leaves rustling; distant music; shouts; etc.
- If you notice that your thoughts have drifted off, then gently return your attention to listening and noticing.
- When the timer sounds, or when you are ready, open your eyes. Consider how you feel, physically and emotionally. Stand up. Stretch.

Reflection: Just noticing (1)

If you keep a journal, you may like to jot down some initial thoughts.

- How long did you spend on the activity?
- What kinds of sounds did you notice?
- What changes did you notice, in your physical or mental state?
- What was the experience like, overall, for you?
- Any other thoughts or observations?

'Just noticing' (2)

Guidance

Time: 10 minutes

- ~ Repeat the 'just noticing' meditation, ideally later on the same day or the following day; don't worry if more time has elapsed.
- ~ Remind yourself of the meditation by reading through the Preparation and Guidance notes on pages 46 and 47 above. You will recall more of the guidance each time, and you will come to remember it.
- ~ Leave enough time to set up and prepare in advance, and to stretch and reflect a little afterwards.
- ~ When the time is up, open your eyes and bring yourself back into the room slowly and quietly. Stretch your limbs.
- ~ Reflect on your experience. Then jot down your observations and reflections.

Reflection: Longer 'Just noticing' (2)

- ~ How long did you spend on the activity?
- ~ What was the experience like?
- ~ How did this compare with last time?
- ~ What do you recall about thoughts and feelings that arose?
- ~ Are there any ways you could set up or prepare differently in order to improve the experience?
- ~ Any other thoughts or observations?

15

Seeing with new eyes

Use this exercise to practise focusing your attention. Notice how much more you take in when you bring your attention to bear, even for the most ordinary objects and the world around you. You may find that you perceive things quite differently by really paying attention to them. This is an easy exercise to draw on in spare moments – or you can add to the time to create a longer meditation.

Preparation

For this exercise, keep your eyes open. Use the preparation notes (page 46).

Guidance

Time: 3–4 minutes

~ Choose a natural object from your surroundings. It could be a leaf, a plant, a piece of fruit, a flower, a seashell, the branch of a tree outside, an insect. It doesn't matter whether you like the item or not.

~ Take two or three minutes just to look, to see it. Be prepared to be patient. Observe the object as if this is the very first time you encountered it. You might notice its outline, its size, the shape it creates in the space around it.

~ Notice whether the object seems to change the more you look at it. Maybe you feel different, or its surroundings appear different. Be aware of the thoughts, feelings, insights that it evokes.

- If you notice that your attention wanders, then just bring it back to the object.
- After 2–3 minutes, take a moment to sit quietly, bringing your attention back to your surroundings gently. Stretch for a moment. Take stock of how you are feeling.
- If you wish, jot down a few thoughts using the reflection below.

 Reflection: Seeing with new eyes

- What did you observe about the object?
- Was this different in any way as the exercise progressed?
- What kinds of thoughts went through your mind?
- Did you maintain your attention on the object? If not, what distracted you? What does that tell you about what is occupying your mind?
- What was the experience like, overall?

Seeing with new eyes (2)

Time: 4–6 minutes

Repeat the exercise above, this time taking a few minutes longer. You can either use the same object or choose a different one.

Afterwards, take a few moments to consider the experience as before, using the reflection above. Jot down a few notes if you wish.

'Laser' concentration

In some traditions, this exercise is used to build a laser-like focus – an ability to really concentrate. If you found the exercise interesting, you might like to repeat it frequently to build your own powers of concentration. It can be very calming. When you become more aware of the world around you, you can find more to admire, respect and enjoy. You recognize just how things change from different perspectives. The same can be true of studying topics in more detail and from several perspectives: you gain a deeper understanding of the whole.

16

Appreciating stillness

Rare jewels

Stillness and silence can be rare experiences. When you start to look for these in your life, you may be surprised at how hard they are to find unless you create the opportunity. We are assailed all the time by noise pollution, media, social media, demands on our attention. You may have noticed this in the previous exercises.

Blocking out the silence

Sometimes this is because we actively avoid circumstances where we may find ourselves alone. Many people are uncomfortable being alone in their own company, in silence. They block out the quiet of their minds by music, games, noise, company, anything rather than just attending to what their minds may have to tell them.

The University of Virginia carried out a study, the findings of which indicated the extraordinary lengths people will go to in order to avoid spending time quietly with their thoughts: 67% of male and 25% of female participants even preferred to give themselves mild electric shocks rather than just do nothing but sit quietly for 6–15 minutes. A third of participants admitted to cheating during the study by looking at their phone. It seems that most people think that doing 'something' is better than doing nothing, even if it causes pain or discomfort (Wilson et al., 2014).

🧘 Reflection: Stillness and silence

- ～ How often do you sit (or stand) in silence, doing nothing except being present with yourself?

- ～ Do you create sufficient opportunities just to 'stand and stare', as you might have done when a child: looking at clouds or a passing aeroplane, feeling the breeze on your face, watching wind move across water or in the leaves of a tree?

- ～ What gets in the way of your doing this more often?

Stillness

Our everyday lives do not normally provide much natural opportunity for just being still. It is easy to spend all of our waking hours racing about to fit in everything we have to do and even searching out distractions so that we don't need to be still. Much of the power of mindfulness comes from stillness:

- From developing the ability to be still when meditating
- From gaining an appreciation of the value of stillness
- From being able to bring stillness and calm to situations as needed.

Activity: Stillness

Consider whether 'stillness' is something you notice much. Do you seek it out? Or avoid it? Or forget you could have more of it?

Below are a number of words, phrases and thoughts associated with stillness. Consider whether any of these have resonance for you. You might like to circle or highlight any that do.

Serenity   **Peacefulness**   **Calm**   **Tranquility**

Relaxation **Focus** **Harmony** **Restful** **Pause**

Quietness **Hush**   **Silence** **Composure** **Softness**

What other words, phrases or situations do you associate with stillness?

Experience it!

Have a go, using the guided exercise below. Enjoy the luxury of doing nothing else but sharing your own company. Observe what happens.

Appreciation of stillness

Guidance

Time: 5 minutes

~ Read through the preparation notes (page 46). Once you have set the timer, aim to maintain stillness. If you need to alter your position, do so by keeping all movements subtle, gentle and to a minimum.

~ Close your eyes. Smile to loosen your face muscles. Then let your face relax naturally.

~ Notice the stillness of your face as a whole, and then each part of your face. You may be able to feel air passing over its surface. If you are frowning or tensing facial muscles in any way, let those muscles relax.

~ Observe the stillness in your body, working from your feet upwards. If you notice any fidgeting or movement, let those areas fall still. Appreciate just being still.

~ By focusing on stillness, you may feel an urge to stretch, yawn, scratch, clear your throat, cough, tap, etc. Aim to resist such urges if at all possible. Focus instead on a part of your body that is still. The urge to move will eventually subside if your attention is focused elsewhere.

~ When the time is up, open your eyes and bring yourself back into the room gently. Stretch your limbs slowly and quietly. Notice how you are feeling. If you wish, jot down your thoughts using the prompts below.

Reflection: Appreciating stillness

~ What was enjoyable? What was challenging?

~ Were you able to maintain stillness? How did this feel?

~ What, if anything, made it necessary to move?

~ Were you able to deflect attention from any urge to break the stillness? If so, were you surprised at how far you could maintain stillness at such times?

~ Any other thoughts or observations?

Appreciation of stillness (2)

Guidance

Time: 10 minutes

~ Read through the Guidance on page 55, and prepare as before.

~ Consider anything that might prompt you to move during the exercise, such as uncomfortable posture, loose hairs tickling your neck, thirstiness, potential interruptions, etc. Address these first.

~ If you have an urge to shift position or break your stillness, see if you can remain calm and still instead. If you must move, do so very slowly, using gentle and subtle movements.

~ Take in the stillness of the room or location. If it is quiet, notice any gentle changes that occur in the stillness, even small, subtle sounds and movements. Notice whether there is any breeze at all, and where you feel it. Is it cool? Warm? Calming? An irritant? Continuous or not? Notice any moments of relative stillness, such as when a noise outside ceases or when people or cars have passed by.

~ Be aware of yourself as part of the stillness. Notice the stillness in your body. Observe yourself noticing the stillness. Let yourself appreciate the stillness. Observe whether you are appreciating the stillness.

~ When the time is up, open your eyes and bring yourself back into the room slowly and quietly. Stretch your limbs. Notice how you are feeling.

~ Jot down your thoughts, using the prompts below.

Reflection: Mindfulness of stillness (2)

~ Were you able to maintain your focus on stillness and silence? What was it like to do this?

~ How did this compare with your experience of this exercise earlier?

~ How still were you? What, if anything, prompted you to move? Were you able to keep any essential movements slow and to a minimum?

~ Any other thoughts or observations?

17

Awareness of body and breath

Self-consciousness about breathing

Although you don't need to change or control your breathing for Mindfulness of Breathing meditation, it is not unusual for people to become a little anxious about their breathing once they focus on it. That is why it is useful to do these short exercises first.

You may notice your breathing slows down or speeds up. If you feel anxious about continuing, you have choices such as one of the following:

- Re-direct attention away from your in-breaths and out-breaths for a while. Choose a new focus, such as your stomach, rising and falling.
- Direct your attention to a part of your body that is less associated with breathing, such as your hands, knees or feet.
- Change to a stillness meditation instead; come back to breathing-related exercises when you feel calmer, or at another time.
- Take a break. There is no need to force the exercise and it doesn't really matter how much you do at any one time.

It is likely that you will get used to paying attention to the breath. After all, you are an expert at breathing already! If you do find Mindfulness of Breathing too difficult, then don't worry. You can use Metta and other exercises instead.

Body and breath exercises

The following exercises are useful to incorporate into the start of all meditation practice, and to return to if you feel discomfort.

Head and shoulders

Awareness of shoulders

Guidance

Time: 2 minutes

- ～ Prepare for the exercise as outlined on page 46.
- ～ Bring your attention to your shoulders. Notice how they rise and fall. Notice whether they rise a little or a lot. Don't try to change the way they move.
- ～ Observe whether you can hear yourself breathing. Don't try to change the way you are breathing. Notice how your shoulders rise and fall in time with your breathing in and breathing out.
- ～ If you notice that your attention has wandered, bring it back to noticing how your shoulders rise and fall as you breathe.
- ～ When you are ready, open your eyes and stretch. Notice how you feel.

Awareness of head and shoulders

Guidance

Time: 3 minutes

- ～ Prepare for the exercise as outlined on page 46.
- ～ As before, bring your attention to your shoulders. Don't change the way you are breathing or moving - just notice your shoulders rise and fall.
- ～ Notice whether your head and neck are relaxed. Does your head feel well supported? If you sense any strain, adjust your position gently.
- ～ Notice whether your head moves when you breathe in and out.
- ～ Notice whether you can hear yourself breathing in tune with movements in your head and shoulders.
- ～ If you become aware that your attention has drifted, bring it back to observing your head and shoulders.
- ～ When you are ready, open your eyes and stretch. Notice how you feel.

Awareness of head, shoulders and tummy

Guidance

Time: 5–10 minutes

- Prepare for the exercise as outlined on page 46. Place your hands on your tummy.

- Observe whether your head and shoulders are comfortable or strained. Adjust your position gently if you are uncomfortable.

- As before, bring your awareness to your head and shoulders. Notice how these move as you breathe. Don't change the way you are breathing – just notice how different parts of your body move subtly as you breathe in and breathe out.

- Bring your attention to your tummy. Observe how it rises and falls as you breathe. Notice how your hands rise and fall on top of your tummy. Notice the pressure of your tummy against your hands.

- Notice whether you can hear yourself breathing as your body fills with air and releases it.

- If your attention wanders, bring your focus back to your tummy rising and falling.

- When you are ready, open your eyes and stretch. Notice how you feel. If you wish, jot down a few reflections.

 Reflection: Head, shoulders and tummy

- What was this like for you, overall? Did you find anything challenging? Did you find it calming?

- How easy was it for you to maintain your focus? What distracted you, if anything?

- Did your breathing change at all during any of these exercises?

- Any other thoughts or observations?

Body sweep

It is easier to maintain longer mindfulness exercises and meditations if your body is relaxed before you begin. This 'body sweep' exercise can be useful before a meditation, as well as before doing exercise, dancing, or going to sleep. If you prefer, you can adapt it to a sitting exercise.

Guidance

Time: 10–30 minutes

Prepare for the exercise as outlined on page 46. Place your hands across your tummy.

1. Lie on the floor, with your head resting on a book, so that your neck is supported and held straight.

2. Bend your knees, keeping these apart and broadly in line with your shoulders; keep your feet flat on the floor.

3. Bring your attention to your toes and relax them, consciously. Do this several times.

4. Bring your attention to your feet, ankles, and your calves, relaxing each of these in turn.

5. Continue to bring your attention up your body from the feet, section by section, through your thighs, buttocks, arms, wrists, hands, fingers, abdomen, chest, shoulders, neck, jaw, mouth, cheeks and eyes.

6. Repeat this, starting again with your feet. This time, sweep your attention more quickly along your body to check that it is relaxed. Bring your awareness to any areas of tension, and let those parts relax.

7. Repeat again. If you are relaxed, this sweep may be faster, but aim to maintain a calm, gentle awareness as you sweep up from your feet.

If you are not well attuned to your body, it may help to contract (tighten) each set of muscles first and then release them gently, so that you are able to notice the difference between feeling tense and relaxed.

18

Mindfulness of Breathing

Mindfulness of Breathing is a very old and powerful meditation. There are various formats that you may encounter depending on what you read or which group you join. Most share the same basic concepts of:

~ Bringing awareness to your breath

~ Noticing the breath rather than aiming to 'control' it.

Some traditions lay more emphasis than others on:

~ Influencing your breathing so that it becomes more subtle

~ Structuring the meditation into stages to sharpen your focus.

The advantages of Mindfulness of Breathing

~ Your breath is always present – you don't need any other kit.

~ It is relatively easy to do whenever and wherever you wish.

~ As breath is essential to life, it is a useful reminder of our presence in the world.

~ A breath does not take long. Its rise and fall is a reminder that all things are in constant flux, coming and going, impermanent.

What it feels like

Although this meditation is simple and repetitive, the experience varies greatly. Some days it can be hard to focus for long at all. At other times, it can feel as if the breath is 'breathing you', drawing you effortlessly into its rhythm. That can be a very peaceful and enjoyable experience.

Mindfulness of Breathing can arouse a profound awareness of being alive, and what it is to exist as a thinking, feeling being. It can also create a strong sense of connection to the world, with an awareness that as you breathe in and out, so do billions of other people and creatures. Experiencing your breathing as a shared activity can generate a feeling of being part of a greater whole. Everyday worries or petty irritations can feel very small in comparison with that sense of being part of a larger community.

Mindfulness of Breathing

Guidance *Time: Start with 5 minutes. Build to 20–45 minutes.*

~ Prepare for the meditation as you did for the Starter Exercises (page 46). Smile gently to relax your face. Keep your mouth slightly open.

~ Begin by tuning in to your body, as you did for *Head, shoulders and tummy* (page 59). Notice whether you are holding tension anywhere. If so, then release it as in *Body sweep* (page 60). If necessary, adjust your position slightly, as in *Appreciation of stillness* (page 55).

~ Bring your attention to your breath. Take a few deep breaths to stabilize your breathing, exhaling slowly. As in *Head, shoulders and tummy*, notice how your body moves in rhythm with the breath.

~ Then notice the first point where the air enters your body on the in-breath. Observe the precise point it makes contact. What does that point feel like as the air passes?

~ Follow the breath as air moves through your nose; maintain your focus on it as it moves along your throat and into your chest. Notice as the air is expelled on the out-breath, and the exact point at which it leaves.

~ Notice how your body moves on the in-breaths, and then the out-breaths. Observe how the various parts of your body all move in concert, as one, as you breathe in and then as you breathe out.

~ If you notice that your attention has drifted onto other thoughts, just bring it back gently to your breath again. The thoughts should drift away. If not, just keep bringing the attention back gently to the breath each time. Let other thoughts just drift away.

~ When the time is up, open your eyes and bring your attention back to the room. Take a few moments to notice how you feel. If you wish, jot down your thoughts and observations.

Mindfulness of Breathing (with counting)

The four-stage, or counting version of Mindfulness of Breathing brings more structure to the meditation. Some people find that this makes it easier, others find it more challenging. Aim to use the Four Stages for the majority of your Mindfulness of Breathing meditations – it develops your focus and patience. For longer meditations, you may prefer either to divide the time equally between all four stages, or to spend longer on the fourth stage.

Guidance   *Time: Start with 10 minutes. Build to at least 20–45 minutes.*

- Prepare for the exercise as outlined on page 46.
- Bring your attention to your body, as for the previous Mindfulness of Breathing meditation. Relax any areas that feel tense.
- Notice whether your mind is preoccupied with any particular thoughts. If so, imagine these drifting away, or stored on a shelf for later.
- Bring your attention to your breath. Take a few deep breaths to stabilize your breathing and watch your breath settle for a few moments.

Stage 1: Counting the in-breaths

In your mind, count out the number '1' just before you breathe in through your nose. Continue to breathe normally. Count '2' just before the next breath begins.

Continue with each in-breath until you reach '9', then start again at '1'.

If your attention drifts, that is to be expected so don't worry about it. Just return your awareness gently to the breath again, starting again from '1'.

Stage 2: Counting the out-breaths

For this stage, count at the end of a complete breath. Count each out-breath from '1' to '9' then start again. Although the timing is not very different, notice how the experience changes.

Some people prefer to count in-breaths; some out-breaths. If you become aware of a preference, aim to equalize your feelings towards both stages.

When counting, do so silently in the space between each breath. If you find that you have to keep beginning from '1' and rarely reach '9', don't be concerned about this. Your focus may be better another day.

Stage 3: Following the complete breath

Follow each breath from start to finish, from when it first enters the body until the end of a complete breath. Do this without counting. Aim to keep your attention focused on the breath continually, in an interested, calm way. If you lose track of the breath, or your attention wanders, there is always the next breath, starting afresh, for you to follow.

Stage 4: Focus on point of entry

Focus your attention just at the very point where the breath enters your body – perhaps the tip or side of a nostril. Observe the sensation of how that feels. Maintain your attention on that point throughout the breath. Expand your awareness to take in all of your body breathing in its steady rhythm whilst you remain focused on the point of entry.

When the time is up, open your eyes and bring your attention back to the room. Take a few moments to notice how you feel. If you wish, jot down your thoughts and observations.

Reflection: Mindfulness of Breathing: Four Stages

- What was this like for you, overall?
- Are there particular stages of the meditation that you prefer?
- How easy was it for you to maintain your focus on counting? Were you able to catch the moments when your attention drifted, returning it to the breath? How did that feel?
- Did you observe any 'inner chatter'? If so, what was the content of this: what were your thoughts?
- Any other thoughts or observations?

19

Managing the challenges of meditation

There is so much positive commentary about mindfulness practice that it can be frustrating if, or when, you find that things don't seem to be going so well for you. If you stay with your practice, it is highly likely that you will feel a wide range of responses, from deep serenity, calm and contentment and even great happiness, through to many negative reactions, too. There will certainly be challenges. Here are typical challenges that you can expect to encounter at some point.

Awareness of the message in the challenge

When we are experiencing frustration, irritation or setbacks, the last thing we might wish to hear is to 'welcome' these. However, all of these provide us with valuable information about ourselves and the world around us. These add to our mental awareness and, ultimately, to our power to adjust our mental attitude or our situation. That is especially the case with meditation.

Typical challenges of meditation

1. Impatience to get back to other things
2. Frustration that your mind keeps wandering
3. Annoyance that you keep losing count of the breaths
4. Distraction by curious, unexpected meditation experiences
5. Disappointment in the immediate experience – it isn't as wonderful as a previous occasion or as other people describe
6. Irritation at the act of counting or even at just sitting
7. A sense of futility, that you feel so unsettled that day, week or month, that meditation feels like 'a waste of time'
8. Exasperation at noises and distractions made by other people
9. Aggravation of sadness or anger that you were feeling already or hadn't noticed you were feeling

10. Dozing off or falling asleep
11. Feeling physical discomfort from the way you are sitting
12. Self-criticism and a judgemental attitude.

1. Impatience to get back to other things

Become aware that you are letting your impatience get in the way of being fully present in the moment. That is something you can address now, for this meditation. Impatience may be something that adds to your stress level generally. When meditating, bring your awareness to your impatience. Acknowledge it. Accept it. Let it subside. Outside of meditation, set aside time to perform some everyday tasks as if in slow motion, noticing the difference of that experience when you are not impatient to complete it.

2. Frustration at the mind wandering

Notice that you are letting yourself get frustrated by something that is normal and to be expected: the mind does wander. The irritation you are experiencing could be a useful signal to you to be more aware of whether you get frustrated unhelpfully with your studies or in life generally. Through meditation, you train yourself to catch your frustration early and to re-focus your attention. This saves you worrying and fretting in place of just doing the things you can do.

3. Annoyance that you keep losing track of the breath

Bring your awareness back to your purpose in counting. Counting is just a tool, a means to an end. When you realize you have lost count, you succeed in catching your attention drifting, and create the opportunity to re-focus it. That is good. Achieving the count of nine doesn't really matter. This can be a good reminder of the importance of not getting so caught up in objectives that you lose touch with the underlying value of experiencing and enjoying the task for what it is.

4. Distraction by curious meditation experiences

It is not unusual to have experiences in meditation that seem amazing, wonderful or odd. These vary hugely from one person to another. It could be anything: a strong visualization that feels like being in a film; a sensation that one side of the body is much bigger than the other, or of heaviness or floating; of bright colours; the sense of having a memory of an event you don't recall, or the sensation of being filled with light and happiness. It is very tempting to cling to these experiences, to try to recreate them, or to look for deep meaning in them. Instead, as always, aim not to grasp after these or to be distracted by them. Hold them lightly. Note them, be prepared to let them go, and focus your attention on the breath. Sometimes, this intensifies the experience further. You will probably find you learn less from such experiences than from other aspects of meditation that seem more of a struggle.

5. Disappointment in the immediate experience

Craving a different experience from the one you are having is one way of not being present in the moment. The intense positive experiences that come from being entirely present in the moment arise from focusing on this moment, right now, fully, so that there is no space for anything else such as wishing for a different experience. Maybe this kind of 'wishing for more' detracts from the pleasure you could take from being more fully absorbed in learning for its own sake. Bring your awareness to ways that you let yourself feel disappointed or let down rather than engaging fully in what you undertake.

6. Irritation at the act of counting or even at just sitting

Just notice this irritation and let it drift away, bringing your attention back gently to the breath. When reflecting afterwards, consider whether such irritation affects how you react to other tasks and situations. Are you sufficiently patient with the process rather than on getting to the end? Are you as open to learning along the way as to achieving a goal?

7. A sense of futility

This can be a useful signal to you that you expect a lot from yourself and situations. When meditating, you have the opportunity to step aside from the need to set objectives, achieve goals or get somewhere. Instead, you have a chance to experience just 'being'. Being with yourself for a few minutes is valuable in itself. Be with you. Experience you. Let yourself enjoy a moment of not having to prove anything.

8. Exasperation at noises and distractions made by others

It can be helpful to us if we can accept noises and distractions made by others as having value, even to our quiet meditation. If our attention has drifted, these can serve as reminders to re-focus it. In some Buddhist cultures, teachers use clashing cymbals, drums and other noise to prevent monks from drifting off during meditations. Our minds have the power to choose how they respond to distraction – as a way of taking us away from our focus, or as a way of bringing us back to it.

9. Aggravation of emotions you were feeling already

Many people come to mindfulness practice with the hope of escaping unwanted emotions and states of mind. Whilst that can happen, it is just as likely that you become more aware of these. That can be useful, in that you can then take steps to deal with them, either through meditation or outside of it. For more about this, see Chapter 46, page 185.

10. Falling asleep

Sleep is a good thing. You may have needed a nap. You might be able to meditate again later. Dozing off is a useful signal that you need to change something. It might be too warm where you are meditating, or the wrong time of day for you, or that you are not getting enough sleep. Often, it is a sign to change your meditation posture (see page 82).

11. Feeling physical discomfort

Take notice of signs of discomfort. These may indicate that you need to adjust your posture, either at that moment through subtle movements, or by setting up your meditation differently next time. (See pages 82–3.)

12. Self-criticism and a judgemental attitude

It is quite typical to get caught up in self-criticism of one kind or another when meditating. This is partly because we are alone with our thoughts and become more aware of things we realize we could do better. It is also partly because we expect mindfulness to be easy, so encountering challenges can take us by surprise. We can lapse into replicating the kinds of self-blaming thought patterns that we bring to other parts of our lives. This can bring some useful personal insights. This is addressed further in the next chapter.

20

Inner chatter and judgemental commentary

During mindfulness practice, we become aware of the commentary that is constantly running through our minds. This may be about study, life, daydreaming, even the meditation itself.

I think this is supposed to make me feel positive but I don't feel positive. I am feeling quite grumpy, actually.

Last time I meditated it felt so lovely. Today, I can't get comfortable. I should sit still. Why does this chair feel lumpy?

That dessert was too sweet. My teeth hurt. When did I last go to the dentist?

Now I feel so calm and centred. This feels amazing. I am brilliant at this meditating. I wonder if I have a special gift for it?

Oh no! Now I am distracted by thinking how brilliant I am – I am not supposed to be focusing on that, am I?

I wonder if I got any 'likes' today.

I'm no good at this. I am sure I'm doing it all wrong …

Was that a pigeon?

I should meditate for longer but I can never stick to it. All the others manage, so I don't know why I can't.

My brain is just too smart for this!

I was very focused there for a while. I wonder if I am better at mindfulness than most people.

I keep forgetting to meditate. I may as well give up.

Oh no! There I go blaming myself just like I am not supposed to do! Failed again! Doh! I'm useless at being non-judgemental!

Inner chatter: 'Do's and 'Don't's

Do ...	Don't ...
• Do notice when you drift into inner chatter and judgement.	• Don't tie yourself up in knots trying to avoid inner chatter and judgement. It will arise.
• Do acknowledge what arises.	
• Do bring your attention back to the breath, as usual.	• Don't dwell on chatter or judgements when they arise.
• Do let go, consciously, of thoughts that return or linger. For example, imagine them floating away like balloons, or stored on a shelf for consideration later.	• Don't fall into further negative self-criticism if you drift into self-judgement.
	• Don't deny or push away the feelings and experiences that arise, or pretend they aren't there – they will bounce back.
• Do keep your response short and simple, to help avoid getting caught up in further distraction or judgements.	• During meditation, don't reflect on the meaning or reasons behind what arises as part of your inner chatter; come back to that afterwards.
• Do respond with kindness and compassion towards yourself. See Metta, page 73.	

👁 Observation: Inner chatter

- ～ Take a few moments after some meditations to jot down the kinds of thoughts, or 'inner chatter', that went through your mind.
- ～ Observe whether your inner script tends to fall into negative self-criticism or self-judgement? If so, what does this consist of?
- ～ How do you deal with these thoughts when they emerge?
- ～ Does your inner commentary fall into blaming and judging others?

It's OK to acknowledge 'negativity'

Noticing negativity

You may notice that your inner commentary is rather negative at times. This may come as a surprise if you had felt you were a positive, well-balanced, 'can-do' kind of person. Alternatively, you may have always assumed you had a negative streak, and it might be tempting now to see this as confirmation of a distorted personality.

Cycles of negativity

Awareness of negativity can prompt a number of further negative reactions, such as:

~ Irritation that everyone else appears so positive

~ Anxiety about being judged and labelled as negative

~ Denying your own reality, pushing away such thoughts and feelings.

This can then feed into a cycle of negativity and self-criticism. If everyone else appears content and cheerful, this might feel isolating, lonely, frustrating or annoying.

Respond equally to whatever arises

It is unrealistic to think you or anyone else should feel positive all the time. It is also unrealistic to assume that bad moods, stress, anxiety or irritation will last forever. You can expect to experience all kinds of emotion and responses, positive and negative, happy and sad, kind and unkind. These are just thoughts. They arise, pass, return, pass again.

Aim to respond in a similar way to whatever arises: just notice it, acknowledge it, let it pass without judging it. So, if you are feeling rather smug about how wonderful you are, acknowledge that: '*I am feeling smug*'. If you are feeling bored with the meditation, acknowledge that: '*I am feeling bored*'. If you are angry and fed up, acknowledge that: '*I am feeling angry and fed up*.' If you feel that your day is going badly, acknowledge that: '*I feel my day is going badly*'.

Shouldn't I try to change?

Recognizing patterns of response

Mindfulness tends to set in train a series of thoughts that prompt and enable you to make changes if you wish. You become better able to recognize particular feelings or thought patterns when they arise in everyday life, and more quickly. This gives you an opportunity to manage your reactions skilfully at an earlier point. As a result, you are better placed to respond differently and as you would wish.

Maintaining calm

Through mindfulness practice, you learn that you can have difficult thoughts and feelings without being overwhelmed by them. You come to know that you can observe yourself naming and noticing your emotions, and that you can breathe through whatever arises. You learn that you can maintain steady breathing, outer stillness and composure, even when experiencing strong emotions. You gain a sense of greater control, so that when the unexpected arises, you know you are able to retain a certain steadiness, calmness and composure.

This doesn't mean you never get surprised nor that you always react as you would wish. However, you are aware of how you could respond, how you did respond, and what to do to help respond as you would wish next time. Over time, this can empower you in managing difficult situations.

'Skilful' and 'unskilful' thinking

Mindfulness is not associated, traditionally, with ideas of 'good' and 'bad'. Such terms suggest an intrinsic, fixed quality. Rather, mindfulness is associated with an awareness that everyone and everything changes all the time – like a river constantly moving.

Instead of 'good' and 'bad' thoughts, which carry a value judgement, you may find it helpful to use the concept of 'skilful' or 'unskilful'. If you are unskilful, you can become more skilful. If you were skilful once, next time you might not be. Your level of skilfulness changes: your practice helps you to develop and nurture skilful responses for more of the time.

21

Metta

Mindfulness and 'Metta'

As we saw in the previous chapter, during Mindfulness of Breathing, we become more aware of the content of our constant inner chatter. This brings us more in touch with things that can be hard for us to deal with:

~ petty resentments and suspicions towards others

~ deep emotions such as anger or rage

~ sadness or shame in realizing we acted badly towards others

~ recognition of failure in managing relationships, finances, study, or just our meditation in that moment.

When such sentiments arise, it can feel natural to indulge in negative responses. This doesn't help. It adds to discontent and unhappiness, and makes it more difficult to really understand and to move on. What is needed is compassion or kindness – but at such times, this can seem extremely difficult to achieve.

Traditionally, practitioners of Mindfulness of Breathing undertook a complementary meditation to help them to manage such responses more skilfully. That practice, known as 'Metta' or 'Metta Bhavana', was used to cultivate kindness and compassion in an active and systematic way.

How Metta practice helps ...

~ It trains you in the ability to generate feelings of warmth, kindness and compassion, even when you aren't in the mood to be generous.

~ When you become aware that you are judging yourself harshly, you are better able to respond with kind consideration towards yourself.

~ When you become aware of difficult feelings, you are better able to sit with them, feeling compassion towards yourself and others. This enables you to deal with them in a non-reactive way.

The ability to feel compassion in difficult moments doesn't usually happen overnight. It is a skill that comes through practice, repeated failure, and more practice. Sometimes, it just involves feeling a bit less angry or resentful. Over time, you recognize the difference this makes.

Metta meditation

Guidance
Time: 20–45 minutes

Take a few moments to prepare (page 46).

This meditation has five stages. You focus on 4 people, one being yourself, and the other three you choose in advance:

- A good friend or person you like or admire
- Someone you don't know well and feel 'neutral' about
- A person that you find difficult or dislike strongly at present.

Stage 1

First, consider how you are feeling about yourself. Whatever this is, bring a feeling of calm, warmth, kindness and compassion towards yourself. If this doesn't come easily, bring a thought or memory to mind that generates a feeling of warmth and serenity. Wish yourself well, repeating a phrase such as 'Let me be well. Let me be happy'. Tune in to your feelings of good will and warmth. Where do you feel them physically? If you can, strengthen that warmth of emotion.

Stages 2–4

After a few minutes, focus on your 'friend' and repeat as above. Then do the same for the 'neutral' person and finally the person you find difficult. It can help to imagine them doing something they enjoy, giving them a gift, watching a sunset with them, simply wishing them peace of mind – anything that generates a sense of warmth and good will towards them.

The aim is to bring the same level of emotion towards all 4 people. This can be difficult. If so:

- Stick with it – don't abandon a stage as an impossible job.
- Bring awareness to a thought that generates good will. Nurture it and then imagine extending it equally to all four people. Repeat a phrase that extends good will towards all – to help nurture the intention.
- Do your best. Even feeling a little more good will is something.

Stage 5

Finally, take a few minutes to extend your feelings of kindness and good will outwards, taking in a wider circle. This might include everyone on your course, the teaching and administrative staff, your family and friends, to everyone you may meet this week – whatever feels right.

When you are ready, open your eyes and take a few moments to come back to the room. If you wish, jot down your thoughts.

Observation 1: Metta meditation

~ What did you observe to be easy or difficult about this meditation?

~ Did you notice differences in how you felt in each stage?

~ Did you make sufficient effort to feel good will and warmth in all stages? If not, what kinds of thoughts got in the way?

~ What thoughts could you bring to mind in order to cultivate warmer feelings and a sense of good will in stages where this was difficult?

Reflection: Metta meditation

Put some time aside occasionally to reflect on your Metta practice.

~ What kinds of thoughts make it easier for you to generate feelings of warmth and kindness?

~ Are there times when you feel 'stuck', such as when you put a particular person in the meditation? Or people you leave out because it then feels too difficult? If so, how can you change that?

~ Are you open to feeling kind towards yourself, or do you resist this?

~ What have you discovered about yourself through this practice?

Self-kindness, or 'metta', when practising mindfulness

Give yourself credit for what you achieve: the time you spend in practice, the changes you experience, the times you notice yourself applying greater awareness or kindness during the day.

Encourage yourself to meditate, rather than forcing yourself to.

Appreciate your experience of mindfulness and Metta practice for what they are. Don't try to force a particular outcome. Don't belittle your experience if others seem to be gaining more from theirs. The experience changes over time for everyone. The greater challenge can lead to greater learning.

Let yourself enjoy the process of meditating and of becoming more mindful.

Let yourself benefit from practising with others, such as through a local mindfulness class or meditation group.

Remain compassionate towards yourself if your mind wanders constantly during meditation. Don't criticize yourself in a negative way. Just return to what you were doing.

Whilst aiming to maintain stillness, don't stay in one position longer than feels reasonably comfortable; gently adjust your position. Experiment with different ways of sitting during meditation. Learn what your body needs.

Consider how your thoughts or actions could be more 'skilled' or 'unskilled' in increasing your awareness and contributing to greater well-being, rather than giving yourself a hard time for getting things 'wrong'.

Appreciate your effort and accept what arises from that. Avoid focusing on what you assume you can't do or didn't do during meditation. Bring your awareness back to the present. What you do now can make a difference.

22

Metta in everyday life

Our responses during meditation tend to mirror how we respond in everyday life. When things don't go our way or we don't feel good about ourselves, it can be difficult to acknowledge how we feel. Such states of mind can make it hard to be generous in our thoughts and actions towards ourselves and others. It can seem much easier just to blame everyone else, the system or the universe!

Things aren't going as I want. Everything is ruined! Why doesn't everyone else notice how terrible this is? I'll make them notice!

Usually, at such moments, generating a feeling of kindness is the last thing we want to do. It can feel much more satisfying to nurture feelings of rage, resentment or revenge. These feelings are not necessarily rational, and they aren't the only way of responding. They certainly don't reduce our feelings of discontent over the longer term. Metta practice helps us manage these impulses and cultivate different emotional habits.

Increasing happiness

Traditionally, the aim of both mindfulness and Metta was to reduce suffering. 'Suffering' may sound rather dramatic, but you can think of it as referring to everything that diminishes our sense of well-being and happiness. That could be major events such as hunger, pain, illness and bereavement. It could also be relatively small things: losing some notes, getting behind with an assignment, missing the bus. Our thoughts influence our emotional response.

Controlling what is ours to control

We can't control everything that goes on around us. Even if we are strong political or social activists or have a job that enables us to make a positive difference in the world, things we don't want and don't like will happen. We will have thoughts we don't want. We will do things we regret. However, we can learn to exercise greater control of ourselves, our thoughts, feelings and actions. Metta practice can help with this.

It starts with a thought ...

How we think affects how we feel: if we think a kind thought, we are more likely to get in touch with a kind feeling.

If we have a kind feeling, we are more likely to respond and behave differently.

From our thoughts, and from small gestures, ripples of change can emerge.

If many people do the same, the ripples become waves.

The totality of our thoughtfulness and kindness affects the amount of unhappiness, confusion or loss there is in the world, for ourselves and for others.

It isn't always easy to really tune in to the feeling of kindness, or to direct this towards some people. The important thing is to go through the process, working on thoughts and feelings during Metta practice. When we do this on a regular basis, it becomes a habit. It becomes easier to connect with feelings of kindness and to notice when these are needed.

🔺 Reflection: Metta for study and everyday life

- ∼ What difference does your Metta practice make to your everyday life?
- ∼ When do you most need to bring kindness to yourself during your studies, or to your experience as a student more generally?
- ∼ What would you change about the way you think or act in order to be kinder to yourself?
- ∼ How might you show more empathy and kindness towards others?

23

Developing your practice

Mindfulness as practice

In order to achieve the mental state associated with mindfulness, you train your mind, over time, through sustained meditation on a regular basis. This is usually referred to as your practice.

The experience of consistent practice can be quite different from that of your first few sessions or of meditating occasionally. You will feel that you are invested differently in the activity and want to give it time, space and energy. It is worth giving more consideration to such things as:

- How long to meditate
- Creating the right space
- Your meditation posture
- Meditating with others
- How to combine meditations
- Managing the time
- Practicalities
- Preparing for a practice session

These are considered below and in Chapter 24.

Building your meditation time

1. There is no need for mindfulness heroics. Don't force it.

2. Start small; build steadily. If you are new to meditation, begin with short meditations of just 5–10 minutes.

3. Build the time gradually to around 20 minutes or so a day.

4. Aim for at least one session a day. Five minutes every day works better than occasional long bursts.

5. You may wish to build to longer meditations of 45 minutes, at least occasionally. These can give a different kind of experience.

6. You can meditate more than once a day if you wish, such as morning and evening.

It isn't necessary to build in long meditations if you don't want to. Little and daily is better than one long session a week. It is the regularity that reinforces the reminders to be mindful outside of meditation practice.

Combining meditations

As you have a choice of meditations and activities, you may wonder which one to choose. The following combinations work well.

Alternating

Ideally, alternate Mindfulness of Breathing and Metta meditations. If you meditate once a day, that means alternating daily. If you meditate twice a day, then you would do both every day, although you may change which you do first each day. Part of your practice is in maintaining a balance, rather than just doing a meditation you prefer.

Aim to stick with the meditation chosen for the session, although you can change over if you feel there is a real benefit.

Drawing across

For longer meditations, where you have more time, it can be useful to spend a few minutes on one meditation before focusing on the second:

- Mindfulness of Breathing settles and focuses you, which can be useful in setting up your Metta meditations.
- Metta meditations remind you to be compassionate towards yourself and others. That can be invaluable if you are in a bad mood or feeling judgemental before Mindfulness of Breathing.

Building in alternatives

Occasionally, replace one of your usual meditations with a walking meditation or focused activity (Chapter 25). This avoids falling into a rut and is a reminder that mindfulness isn't just about sitting on cushions.

> **👁 Observe: Which meditation?**
>
> Notice whether you feel differently towards one meditation or another?
>
> How does this affect the way you approach the practice?

Creating the right space

Set up a welcoming space

You can alter the quality of your practice through the way you arrange your space. You don't need anything special, but you may find it helpful to create an ambiance that orientates you quickly into a receptive state of mind for meditation. Aim for a space that reflects how you want your mind to be – such as calm, clear and uncluttered.

Fresh air, tidiness and general cleanliness make the space feel cared for, and that you matter. Clear away any mess in the immediate area.

A small mat is useful for designating meditation space, at least during meditation times. You might like to add pictures or flowers.

Aim for quiet. Remove distractions from the area. If you live in student accommodation, leave a note not to be disturbed.

Adjust the lighting to suit you, whether bright and airy, or dim and atmospheric. If permitted by your building's fire regulations, a candle provides a good focus before starting your meditation.

Arrange the cushions or chair so that they help you maintain your meditation posture (page 82). It can take a while to adjust these so that you find the optimum position and feel comfortable, especially at first. It is fine to improvise with rolled up towels or jumpers instead of cushions, if these are what you have to hand.

♟ Reflection: Your meditation space

~ Is your meditation space set up as you would like it?
~ When you walk near the meditation space during the normal course of the day, does it create a positive reminder about meditation, encouraging you to meditate?
~ If not, how might you change it so that it is more inviting?

Posture for seated meditations

Posture is important for maintaining stillness and alertness. If you are too rigid, you will get uncomfortable more quickly; if you are too relaxed, you may slump into sleep. There are various postures that you can take – these being two of the most commonly used. If these don't work for you, adapt them so you are comfortable.

Tailor position

- ～ Sit on one or more firm cushions
- ～ Knees touching the floor (adjust cushion height to help)
- ～ Or knees resting on cushions
- ～ One foot tucked in close to the body
- ～ The other foot resting just in front of it
- ～ Hands resting on knees or in lap.

Seated on chair

- ～ Sit straight-backed near the front of chair
- ～ Or with a cushion behind your back
- ～ Feet flat on the floor or cushion
- ～ Hands resting on cushion.

Whatever your posture, aim to be:

- ～ Relaxed but upright, as if being drawn upwards gently
- ～ Shoulders down and relaxed
- ～ Stomach relaxed and sticking out
- ～ Eyes forward, open or closed
- ～ Ideally mouth closed, jaw relaxed
- ～ Maintaining a hint of a smile can help relax the face.

Practical considerations

Diary management
Designate a time each day for meditation. If you need to change it, make sure you designate a new time.

Food Give some thought to how much you eat just before a meditation. Too much may make you sleepy; too little and you may be distracted by hunger or a rumbling tummy.

Clothes Check whether your clothes will constrain or distract you: you may wish to avoid anything itchy or scratchy. It is usually better to take off your shoes for sitting meditations.

Managing the time

It can be hard to judge time when meditating: it can rush by or crawl slowly. You could set an alert using a timer to avoid distracting thoughts about time. If you are meditating with others, you could take it in turns to be time-keeper instead. A bell, gong, or gentle tapping on a book can bring people back to the room more gently than a timer.

Extending or shortening your session

If you want to extend your meditation, that is fine. If you sit for a long time, be mindful of your posture and that you are not forcing yourself through physical discomfort. If a meditation feels disappointing or frustrating, it can be tempting to abandon it early. It is better to work with these feelings if you can, even if it seems a waste of time. Ultimately, it is working with the difficult meditations that leads to the greatest long-term gains. On meditation challenges, see pages 65–8.

Preparing yourself for meditation

Orientate yourself towards meditation

The way you set up your practice can affect how it will go. Your practice
really begins before you sit down to meditate. When it is feasible, start to
power down beforehand, so that your head isn't buzzing with things you
feel you must do. Observe how long you need in order to feel composed
in mind and body for the start of your practice.

Create a sense of unpressurized time

The way you use the time before and after it can make meditation time
feel calmer or pressurized. Organize your time well so that you are not
rushed in preparing and setting up in advance, and for ending the
meditation calmly. Give yourself the sense of having plenty of time.

*Avoid rushing in at the last minute, head buzzing, and crashing onto your
cushions.*

Ending the meditation well

Just as it helps to set up your meditation well, it also matters how you end
it. Don't just rush away. Take a few moments to take in the meditation.
Stretch, and re-orientate yourself back into your day. If you have time, take
a few moments to reflect on what you can take from the meditation into
your day. Clear your meditation space slowly, with awareness, to bridge
practice time with the rest of your day.

24

Meditating with others

Most of your practice is likely to be undertaken on your own, in your room. This is excellent discipline but it can take lots of will power to maintain daily meditation without continued input from others. It really helps to find one or more people to meditate with from time to time. Many practitioners attend a group session at least once or twice a week.

The advantages

Community, sharing and experience
1. The experience is different when there is a room of people all focused on meditating.
2. Groups provide a useful sense of community and solidarity.
3. It is good to have people you can talk to about your experience and thoughts. Even if their experiences are not identical to yours, they will understand the context.
4. It can be a pleasant way of socializing and making friends.

Motivation
5. The presence of others is good motivation to turn up, stay with the meditation to the end of the session, and to stick with meditation generally.
6. When others are present, you can tend to settle into meditation more quickly, rather than continuing to find the perfect arrangement for your seating or making the space feel right.

Technique
7. You pick up useful tips on posture, breathing, reading, websites, classes.
8. You hear about other people's experiences, which provides a context for interpreting your own experience and helps maintain a sense of perspective when needed.

9. When others are meditating nearby, this serves as a good reminder to keep any essential movements small and subtle, and to refine your breathing, as you do not want to disturb others.

Finding a group

There are lots of groups that you can join. Your college or university counselling services or student support services will probably know of local groups and may even run some on campus. Otherwise, look out for advertisements for groups in local cafés that have community noticeboards, or ask at the nearest community centre. Health shops and sometimes doctors' surgeries can be useful sources of information about local groups.

Each group has a different atmosphere. If there are several groups to choose from, try them out a few times to find the one you prefer.

⚓ Reflection: Meditating with others

~ How does your own experience vary depending on whether you meditate alone or with others?

~ If you don't currently spend any time in meditation with others, how might this benefit you?

25

Mindfulness in everyday activities

Almost anything can be used as an opportunity for practising mindfulness. You may find that everyday activities are transformed when looked at as meditative acts. This is especially so for actions that you usually find boring or annoying or that you imagine offer little to observe. When you direct your attention to them so that you can really take in what is happening, you notice all kinds of things that you would normally miss.

A great example of this is provided by the Vietnamese Buddhist monk Thich Nhat Hanh (1988) in his description of watching apple juice becoming clear liquid as the sediment settles. For him, this exemplifies the way that the mind itself becomes clear as thoughts settle during meditation.

Turning ordinary occurrences and everyday actions into meditations can provide a useful and important bridge for applying, and absorbing, mindfulness into your everyday life. You may see immediate benefits from adopting this for study tasks that require attention to detail, such as checking citations and referencing, or editing and proof-reading your work.

For this exercise, it is really up to you what you choose. Actions that you undertake on a regular basis provide a good place to start, such as:

~ mindfulness when walking

~ mindfulness when eating

~ mindfulness when queuing

~ mindfulness when travelling.

Have a go, using the principles and guidelines provided below. Then choose any other areas that draw your attention.

General principles for mindfulness in everyday activities

Duration. Choose an activity that can last at least a few minutes.

Single activity. Don't combine the activity with any other: let yourself focus fully on what you are doing.

Take your time. Don't rush the activity. Be present in each second.

Go slow. Slow your movements down a little, as if you were in slow motion or at least not rushing the activity as you might do as a rule. This will enable you to take in things that you might not notice, usually.

No 'goal'. Apart from objectives intrinsic to undertaking the task and being mindful, don't seek a particular outcome. Don't aim to complete the task better, faster, with more fun, with a great attitude, etc. Just focus fully on each action in each moment.

Take notice. Bring your focus to each aspect of the task in turn. Really notice what you are doing, what the action feels like physically, how you react to different aspects, how you feel, etc. Use all your senses.

Likes and dislikes. Notice whether you have feelings of aversion: things you don't like, don't want to do or want to put off. Conversely, notice any feelings of 'craving': whether you are eager to stop, rush, keep going, do something different, drink, eat, etc.

Notice changes of attitude. Observe whether your attitude towards the task, or any aspect of it, changes as a result of altering your approach to it. What feels different?

Mindfulness when walking

This is a great meditation to do if you need a break from sitting. You can incorporate meditation into walking across campus, to the shops, or around the library. You can walk back and forth in straight lines across your room or round the periphery, or take a walk outside for a break.

Preparation

Decide your route. If you are in your room, clear furniture to make space, or create a route around it.

Guidance   *Time: 5–20 minutes*

- Bring your attention to where you are placing your feet. Notice how it feels as you raise them and as they make contact with the ground.

- Notice where you feel the movement in your body.

- Notice your attitude to the task of walking: does it change?

- Notice your surroundings as you walk.

- Notice whether you are drifting into setting goals, such as how much longer to keep walking? Whether to achieve a particular number of steps to help your fitness routine? Covering a particular distance? Checking something quickly whilst passing by? Trying to calm down? Thinking through the solution to a problem? If so, just bring your attention back gently to being present in each moment, step by step.

Reflection: mindfulness of walking

- How long did you spend on the activity? Was this what you intended?
- What was the experience like?
- What was different about walking when you brought your attention to it in this way?
- Any other thoughts or observations?

Mindfulness when eating

You can do this for any meal. The first few times, you may prefer to do this when eating somewhere quiet on your own.

Guidance

Time: 5–20 minutes

~ First, notice how the food is arranged, and whether it looks appealing. Take in its aroma. Notice your responses.

~ Prepare a mouthful of food. Notice how you select it, cut it and ready it to eat. Observe how your body starts to anticipate the first mouthful.

~ Let a small mouthful of food rest on your tongue for a moment. Observe how it feels in your mouth.

~ Observe how you chew and swallow; how fast or slowly you eat; the parts of your face that are involved as you eat.

~ Notice how the food tastes, and how the taste changes.

~ Be aware of your attitude as you eat. Are you tempted to rush through it or to savour your food? Is there anything you don't want to eat or that you enjoy more on the plate? Do you eat your favourite foods first, save them until last, or eat them along with everything else?

~ Notice if you drift into setting goals, such as counting calories, finishing quickly, or promising yourself dessert if you eat your vegetables!

~ Observe whether you drift into self-criticism – maybe about an aspect of how you eat, what you eat, your size, your shape, your attitude to food?

~ If you notice your attention has drifted, just bring it back gently to eating.

> ### Reflection: Mindfulness of eating
>
> ~ What was different about the experience of eating when you brought your attention to it in this way?
> ~ What kinds of things did you observe?

Mindfulness when waiting in line

Waiting in line, or queuing, can be a frustrating activity but it doesn't need to be. It can be a good opportunity to meet new people or catch up with friends. It can also be a great chance to practise mindfulness.

Guidance

Time: 5–20 minutes

~ Bring your attention to your initial reaction to having to wait in line. What emotions does it evoke? Notice whether you are still holding onto that reaction; if so, just let it go.

~ Bring your awareness to your breath. Observe it for a few moments, as in Mindfulness of Breathing meditation. Let it calm.

~ Bring your attention to any sense of impatience. That won't make the line move faster. Let it go.

~ Observe whether you are straining to see if the queue is moving, tapping your feet, or showing signs of irritation. Let yourself be calm and still as you wait. Appreciate the chance just to be alive, still, breathing, occupying a moment in time.

~ Notice how you are feeling towards others who are waiting. Remember your Metta practice: see if you can bring feelings of compassion towards them. They are held up, waiting, just like you. That may cause them difficulties later.

~ When your time queuing is over, notice how you are feeling. If you can, bring gratitude to the queue for enabling a moment of awareness.

Reflection: Waiting in line

~ What was different about waiting in line when you brought your attention to it in this way?

~ Did you notice any changes to your attitude, mood or behaviour?

Mindfulness when travelling

When you are travelling, the journey can sometimes seem to go too slowly. It can be easy to get impatient and to wish the journey away, rather than just being fully present in it. Journeys provide good opportunities for engaging in some mindfulness practice.

Guidance

Time: 5–20 minutes

~ Bring your attention to your feelings about the journey. Acknowledge that you are having those feelings.

~ Notice whether you are impatient about the journey, such as wishing it over quickly. If so, observe the emotions that it evokes. Let go of these.

~ Bring your awareness to the fact that you are in transit between two places, and how that feels.

~ Bring your attention to your surroundings. Notice where you are, who is around you, what kinds of things there are to observe. Let your attention take in each of these things fully without getting drawn into thinking about them. Direct your attention to its next focus point.

~ When your journey ends, bring your awareness to the opportunity it gave you for being mindful. Observe how you feel.

Reflection: Travelling

~ How did you incorporate mindfulness into your journey?

~ What was the effect of this on your experience of the journey?

~ How else might you incorporate mindfulness or Metta into your daily travel or into long journeys?

26

Bringing mindfulness into everyday life

Wanting to be mindful

Whether or not you intend to bring mindfulness and Metta into your studies and everyday life, it is likely that these will seep into your way of thinking if you maintain your practice. You can accelerate and intensify that process by actively seeking to be more mindful. That is largely a question of intent – or wanting to bring a more conscious or wakeful mind to bear on how you are in the world.

It is highly unlikely that you will achieve the full potential of mindfulness straight away. The achievement of full and sustained mindfulness is rather elusive for most people. Indeed, part of becoming more mindful is that you start to recognize how unaware we are for most of the time. It is more realistic to think about having an intention to become *more* mindful.

Taking action to be mindful

As well as developing your daily meditation practice, there are other things that you can do to be more mindful during the course of the day. This chapter looks at three of these:

~ Two-minute meditations

~ Deliberately Mindful Moments (DMMs)

~ Taking care of your mind.

Two-minute meditations

The beauty of two-minute meditations is that they can be inserted at any point in the day, almost anywhere, without preparation. They provide a great way of bridging formal meditation practice and everyday life.

The trick is to spot occasions in the day when you can take about two minutes to focus on your breath or on developing feelings of kindness towards yourself or others. Ideal moments tend to be where there is a natural or unexpected pause in activity, such as those below.

Good opportunities for a two-minute meditation

Whilst waiting for your laptop to boot up

When looking out of a window

Whilst a lecturer is setting up their lecture

Waiting for the kettle to boil

Waiting for toast to come out of the toaster

When you are waiting for someone to arrive

When waiting for a friend to complete a phone call

When standing in queues

🧘 Reflection: Two-minute meditations

~ What kind of occasions arise for you that would lend themselves naturally to a two-minute meditation?

~ What would help you to remember to do this?

Deliberately Mindful Moments (DMMs)

DMMs are different from two-minute meditations in that you simply decide to bring a greater intensity of awareness to a particular moment. You can make these as long or as short as you like – a few seconds or several minutes. You can bring your focus to anything, such as

~ How your hands move across the keyboard when you type

~ The act of putting on a piece of clothing

~ Each action that goes into brushing your teeth

~ Your actions as you sit down and ready yourself for study

~ How you react when others waste time in class

~ Closing a door silently, using the handle.

Guidance

Bring a more focused awareness to what, precisely, you are doing. It can help to slow down your action, so that you can notice more. Observe what is different about the task when you are fully focused on every aspect of it.

~ Let yourself appreciate each aspect of the task and the sense of undertaking it in a thoughtful, purposeful, conscious way.

~ Observe the precise movements you make – with your fingers, hands, arms, feet, head; how your body is moving. Bring attention to how each separate movement starts, continues, completes, leads into the next or follows from what came before.

~ Notice your attitude towards different aspects of the task.

~ Notice whether your body feels relaxed or calm; check whether your face feels relaxed, especially around your mouth and jaw.

♟ Reflection: Deliberately Mindful Moments

~ What did you observe as different about the task during the DMM?

~ When might you bring your focus to what you are doing in this way?

~ What would help you to remember to do this?

Taking care of your mind

Practitioners of mindfulness come to value mental alertness. They appreciate the benefits of being able to move, at will, into a deliberately heightened awareness of what they are thinking, doing and feeling – or 'meta-awareness'. To give themselves the freedom to adopt such states when they wish, they take care of their mind and body. You may wish to consider these for your own practice.

For a clear, focused mind ...

~ Gain sufficient sleep so that the mind is alert when awake.

~ Avoid any substances such as alcohol, cigarettes, or unprescribed drugs that might dull or distort your thought processes, both in general and especially just before meditation.

~ Meditate at times when you are most likely to feel awake and alert.

Contents of the mind

Your mind creates images and new thoughts from what you feed it. If your mind is preoccupied with art, it generates art. If it is preoccupied with arguments or fights, it busies itself with these. If you supply it with a constant stream of violent images, frightening thoughts and scary plots, then you can expect it to make a meal with these ingredients. The same is true of thoughts that create anxiety, worries, guilt. What you feed the mind will be fed back to you in dreams, meditations, and in the thoughts and emotions you experience across the day.

Meditation can make you more sensitive to things that you see, hear and focus on, as you become more aware. You may find that your sleep and dreams become more sensitive to the content of television, videos and games, especially if these are violent or frightening.

If you notice this, and it makes you feel uncomfortable, then do take more care of what you expose your mind to.

27

Tips on technique

Schedule daily slots

Put time aside in your diary at least once every day for the next three months for your mindfulness practice. Ideally, make this for the same time every day, although if you can't do that, any time is better than none. If you miss a session, aim to fit it in later in the day, even if for only a few minutes.

Leave additional time if you can

You can gain even more from practice sessions and from study if you have time to prepare a little in advance, and to stay with your thoughts for a few moments afterwards. Allowing this extra time means you can continue for a bit longer with an exercise or meditation that you are enjoying or from which you feel certain benefits.

Keep it simple

Avoid over-complicating or over-thinking it. Consider whether making any changes to your practice would help, but don't worry about whether you are sitting 'correctly' or 'doing it right'.

No goals

Don't set out to achieve a particular goal or outcome from practice sessions. Be open to what arises.

No blaming

Don't beat yourself up if things don't go to plan. Be open to what arises next time. It may be very different. See Chapter 20.

Avoid grasping

Don't try to hold onto thoughts and insights during meditation. Practise is not, itself, a reflective exercise. Trust that these will come back to you later if they are really important.

Start with a smile

You don't have to do this. However, it does relax facial muscles and can reduce tension in the jaw. It uses fewer facial muscles than frowning. Smiling releases 'happy chemicals', which can help you feel more contented during the mindfulness session – and when studying.

Stick with your time

Whatever time you set, aim to stay with the meditation at least until that time is up. It develops good habits – for meditation as well as for sticking with study and work tasks too. Meditating longer is fine if it feels right.

Practise alongside others

It makes a difference to share the experience. See pages 85–6.

Persevere

You are training your mind to develop new skills and habits. As with any skills and habits, the benefit comes from practice and time.

28

FAQs about technique

What if I can't maintain a sitting posture?

If there are medical reasons why you cannot maintain a sitting posture, use a walking meditation instead. See page 89.

Why can I only manage a few seconds being focused before I get lost in thought for the rest of the meditation?

That is to be expected from time to time, especially when meditating alone. Joining a group or class can help. If you persevere and you find you haven't been able to notice that your attention has drifted, then break your session into shorter slots. Set a timer to sound every few minutes, or whatever you find useful. Alternatively, be alert to a particular sound that is likely to occur frequently in your vicinity, such as doors closing or cars passing. Each time you notice that sound, use it as a reminder to bring your attention back to the breath or the focus of your meditation.

What if I prefer one kind of meditation practice more than another? Can I just stick with that?

It isn't ideal as the Mindfulness of Breathing and Metta meditations are complementary. Ultimately, it is your choice: nobody will know what is going on in your mind. However, do aim to persist. Observe the effects of different meditations, and decide whether such effects are beneficial, even if you find the practice difficult or you feel aversion to it. Decide what you want from your practice: the most profound effects aren't necessarily gained from what you find easiest or most enjoyable. (see 'Combining meditations', page 80).

I am not noticing anything happening during meditation – should I?

Your attention is on your breath or whatever is the focus of the meditation. That is what you will notice. Apart from that, you may not notice anything in meditation. You may, at times, come to feel a wide range of things, as outlined on pages 26 and 65.

- ~ Mindfulness acts in a paradoxical way: if you chase after results, it becomes harder to be present in the moment, which is an important part of the practice. It reduces the impact.
- ~ It is possible that you haven't been practising on a regular basis for long enough. You may just need to practise more.
- ~ Consider how you set up your practice – it may help to spend more time powering down and creating the right ambiance (page 84).

I have been meditating for a few weeks. I don't feel any different? Am I doing something wrong?

If you are following the guidance, it is likely that you are not doing anything wrong. Sometimes changes are subtle so you don't notice them straight away. You may gain more from joining a class led by a teacher and having other people around to share details of their experience.

I don't really feel any kindness or compassion during Metta meditations even when I try. What can I do?

It can be really challenging, which is why Metta meditation is so valuable. Don't force a particular feeling but aim to be creative in generating a spark of warmth, or a way of sharing good will. It can help to do one or more of the following:

- ~ Think about something or someone that you care about first.
- ~ Bring to mind a happy memory.
- ~ Imagine a scenario in which people are happy or where you feel good, such as being on holiday, a sunny day, a walk by the sea, a meal with friends, people laughing together.
- ~ Repeat phrases that represent good will, such as 'Let X be happy. Let X be well and healthy', even if you don't yet feel them. Focus on what those words mean and let your mind absorb that.

Sky-like mind

To assist their practice,
traditionally, meditators
imagine that their mind
is like a clear blue sky.

When you think about such
a sky, it provides a mental
focus that is clear of clutter.

The image of a deep blue
sky, clear of clouds and
obstructions, can be
uplifting.

It also provides
a clear backdrop
which helps you notice
when thoughts arise –
so you can let them drift away
gently like clouds.

You might like to try this
when you are meditating,
or when just sitting quietly.

NB This is not the same as 'blue sky' thinking as referred to in business contexts. Blue sky thinking has the aim of generating new ideas. Although new and creative ideas often do arise when you have a 'sky-like' mind, that is not the purpose.

Part
3

Applying mindfulness to study

29

Applying mindfulness to study

If you would like your studies to be more enjoyable, less stressful and more effective, then mindfulness is one way of achieving that. This section looks at ways that you can be more mindful in the natural course of your study, applying what you learn from regular mindfulness practice.

Seven ways of applying mindfulness to study

There are all kinds of ways that you could apply mindfulness to support your study. Here are seven key ways of doing so.

1. Setting up your day mindfully for more effective study
2. Using meditation practice as an anchor point in your day
3. Using a mindfulness 'warm-up' just before sitting down to study
4. Increasing your awareness of attention lapses during study
5. Taking a more mindful approach to study
6. Bringing kindness, or 'Metta', to your studies
7. Applying mindfulness to specific everyday study tasks.

More details of these are provided below and in the chapters that follow. When you have started to develop the habit of drawing on mindfulness and Metta, you will find many more ways of applying these to other aspects of your study, and to your life in general.

Growing your awareness

During mindfulness practice, it is likely that you will notice that when your attention drifts, certain kinds of thoughts recur. These are useful indicators of such things as:

- ~ The things you don't want to do, including study tasks
- ~ The things you really want from life and study
- ~ The excuses you are trying to create
- ~ Who or what you are trying to blame.

1. Set up your day mindfully for more effective study

Every morning, you have an opportunity to set the tone for an effective day's study. Once you have completed your meditation or a mindfulness exercise, you will be in a better state of mind to focus on what you want from your day's study.

If you can't set up a morning meditation, you can bring mindfulness to one or more activities you normally undertake, from brushing your teeth, to eating breakfast or travelling to campus. After doing so, take two or three minutes to consider such things as:

- ～ The kinds of study tasks you will engage in today – whether reading in the library, writing an assignment, attending lectures, and so on
- ～ Where the challenges will lie in staying focused on your study today
- ～ What you will do to maintain your focus
- ～ How you could be just a little bit better at your study today
- ～ How you will find enjoyment and pleasure in today's study.

2. Use meditation practice as an anchor point in your day

If you set up a meditation practice as outlined in Chapter 23, this can have an anchoring effect on your time. Your meditation slot provides a fixed point in the day around which you can schedule other things. This is especially useful for those things you mean to do but which tend to get forgotten – such as reading for pleasure, exercise, relaxation, reflection, setting up your day, or calming down before sleep.

Using meditation as such an anchor can bring calm and focus to your day – and a greater sense of your priorities.

3. Use a mindfulness 'warm-up' just before studying

Settle and re-focus your mind just before studying by using a short 'warm-up'. This is especially useful when studying on your own or for study tasks that you expect to be especially challenging. See page 111.

4. Increase your awareness of attention lapses during study

Being mindful involves being aware of how your mind wanders. In a learning context, this includes becoming more conscious of where your attention tends to drift when you are studying. Knowing that helps you to set up your day and organize study sessions so that you are better placed to study more effectively. See the self-evaluation on pages 109–10, and Chapters 37–8 on multi-tasking.

5. Take a more mindful approach to study

The mindset or attitude that you bring to study affects the tone of your study, making it easier or more difficult to engage fully, to find it enjoyable, and to stick with difficult tasks. Consider the mindset you bring currently to study, especially to tasks you don't like and to situations that aren't going as well as you hoped.

Become more aware of how your thoughts and actions might undermine your enjoyment of study and its effectiveness. See pages 123–42.

6. Bring kindness, or 'Metta', to your studies

Studying can be tough and stressful. It is easy to fall prey to negative self-criticism. Become more aware of:

- ~ times when you need to be kinder towards yourself

- ~ how and when you put yourself under unnecessary pressure

- ~ the way you act towards yourself and others when things get tough

- ~ how you can build better habits of consideration towards yourself and others, to benefit your study and well-being. See pages 113–14.

7. Apply mindfulness to specific everyday study tasks

The study process is composed of many discrete study tasks, all of which can benefit from greater awareness of how you approach them. Part 3 looks at core study tasks to which you can bring a more mindful approach. This will enable you to develop the habits and mindset to apply to any other aspect of your study or experience as a student.

Reflection: Applying mindfulness to study

- ~ Give some initial thought to these seven ways of applying mindfulness.
- ~ Imagine fitting some, or all, of these into your week. Which do you consider would be the most useful for you to begin with?

Mindfulness of attention lapses

Identify which of the following apply to you. Indicate the frequency of each, on a scale from 'Never' to 'A lot' (e.g.: *Never - - - - X- - A lot*).

Aspect	Frequency
I find it hard to focus my attention when I first sit down to study	*Never - - - - - - - A lot*
I find it hard to maintain attention when I haven't eaten a good meal recently	*Never - - - - - - - A lot*
I find my attention wanders if I am tired	*Never - - - - - - - A lot*
I find it harder to concentrate at certain times (e.g. late at night)	*Never - - - - - - - A lot*
I find it harder to concentrate in certain locations (at home, some seats in the library)	*Never - - - - - - - A lot*
I find it harder to maintain attention when I am not enjoying what I am doing	*Never - - - - - - - A lot*
I find it harder to maintain attention if I am finding the work difficult	*Never - - - - - - - A lot*
I keep interrupting what I am doing, to attend to different study tasks – or other things	*Never - - - - - - - A lot*
I check messages, texts, etc. frequently rather than at times I set aside to do this	*Never - - - - - - - A lot*
I waste time on tasks that are not essential, even when I am short of time	*Never - - - - - - - A lot*
I am often late when I mean to be on time	*Never - - - - - - - A lot*
I miss appointments or lessons	*Never - - - - - - - A lot*
I forget to write all the information that I need into my diary/planner	*Never - - - - - - - A lot*
I find I am thinking about things other than the task I am supposed to be working on	*Never - - - - - - - A lot*

Aspect	Frequency
I get distracted by wondering what other people are doing or thinking	*Never - - - - - - - A lot*
I often get to the end of a page without being able to recall what I have read	*Never - - - - - - - A lot*
When reading, I get to the end of a chapter without being aware of its key themes	*Never - - - - - - - A lot*
I read through my notes repeatedly to revise material, without really taking it in	*Never - - - - - - - A lot*
I get bored with study tasks quickly	*Never - - - - - - - A lot*
I assume things are boring, or 'not me', rather than searching out their points of interest	*Never - - - - - - - A lot*
When writing, I go off at tangents, forgetting the title of the assignment	*Never - - - - - - - A lot*
I become over-absorbed in what I have to say, forgetting the original question	*Never - - - - - - - A lot*
I multi-task during lectures and seminars – e.g. checking my phone, using social media	*Never - - - - - - - A lot*
I become preoccupied with study when I should be doing other things	*Never - - - - - - - A lot*
I worry about study when I should be asleep	*Never - - - - - - - A lot*

🧘 Reflection: Lapses in my attention

Considering your answers above:

~ When are you most at risk of drifting off task, finding it hard to focus or to maintain concentration?

~ What is the effect of these attention lapses?

~ What is it about the way you set up or approach the study task that contributes to lapses of attention to your studies?

Check through the relevant chapters below to identify ways you could apply mindfulness to improve your attention to study tasks.

30

Mindful 'warm-up' to study

Use a short pre-study meditation as a 'warm-up' for your mind, just as you would warm up before doing strenuous exercise. You can do this before any class or independent study session. It is especially useful if you have focused reading to do, or if you are writing an assignment, working on maths problems or doing creative work.

Guidance

Time: 5–10 minutes just before study

~ Choose your meditation. This could be Mindfulness of Breathing, Metta, a walking meditation, or other exercises outlined in Part 2. Decide which would most benefit your study in this moment.

~ Appreciate the meditation or exercise for its own value, as time set aside to prepare your mind for the study task ahead.

~ Focus on the meditation – your breath if you are doing a Mindfulness of Breathing, your walking if that is the focus. Your aim at this point is just to maintain that focus – not to think ahead about what you are going to do with the study task. There is time for that afterwards.

~ However, as this is a 'warm-up to study' meditation, if your mind wants to leap ahead and get on with study, great! Go with the energy to study. You can always take a few minutes later to 'warm up' again if needed.

Things to watch for ...

~ Whether you are trying to 'race through' the warm-up meditation in order to get on with study. It is good if you are now keen to get on with your study – although in general, be mindful of meditation when meditating, and studying when studying, rather than looking ahead.

~ Whether you found it easy or difficult to remain focused during the warm-up and what kinds of things distracted your attention.

~ Whether your attitude, or state of mind, is suitable for the study session you are about to engage in.

Respond to what you notice during 'warm-up'

If you notice that you are highly distractible or preoccupied, it might be a good idea to take steps to address this. For example:

~ removing distractions from the area

~ making sure you have what you need to study

~ considering whether you need to deal with whatever is preoccupying or distracting your mind before starting to study – sorting out an urgent task; eating if you are hungry; changing your clothes if they feel uncomfortable for study; getting a drink if you are thirsty, etc.

~ doing some exercise, or even some housework if you live at home, to work off excess adrenalin

~ tuning in to an aspect of your motivation for study, such as your curiosity about something you are about to read, or interest in what you might discover

~ dividing your study into shorter sections so that you can retain a better focus on each.

👁 Observation: 'Warming up' for study

~ What is your attitude, typically, towards doing the pre-study 'warm-up': do you welcome it or resist it?

~ Do you stay focused during the warm-up?

~ How do you feel after the warm-up meditation?

~ What do you observe about your attitude towards settling down to study after a warm-up meditation?

🔔 Reflection: 'Warming up' for study

When you have tried this a few times, jot down your observations and insights.

~ When is it most useful for you to do a warm-up meditation?

~ Does it improve your concentration?

~ Do you gain anything else from it?

31

Applying 'Metta' to study

Many students would benefit from a little more self-kindness and self-compassion. The ways in which you go about your study can add greatly to its inherent challenges and difficulties. That includes such things as:

Unrealistic self-expectations Pushing towards unreasonable goals, rather than being inspired by good, aspirational ones

Catastrophizing Assuming that all future success hinges on a particular degree or grades rather than considering the multiple options that are available now or that can be created across a lifetime

Narrow-mindedness Limiting options by deciding something is not for you, is 'boring', that your opinion must be right, that you already know everything or that you can't learn in a particular group, rather than being open to possibilities, and taking more responsibility to make things work

Over-extending Taking on too many things at once, making disappointment or failure more likely

Overlooking great learning opportunities Being self-critical or blaming others when things don't go brilliantly, rather than focusing on the valuable lessons to take away from experience.

All these, and many more that you can probably think of, contribute to making study more difficult than it needs to be.

👁 Observation 1: Self-kindness and study

1. How does your approach to study add to pressures you are under?
2. How could you be kinder to yourself in the way you think about study or organize your life around it?
3. Do you ever drive yourself to achieve, to the extent that you lack compassion for what your mind, body or feelings really need? If so, how does that lack of self-kindness manifest itself?
4. Does the way you approach your studies mean you end up being unnecessarily unkind to others?
5. Jot down your observations and reflect upon these. What do they tell you about yourself and your approach to your study?

Self-kindness for mindful study

Don't focus on what you haven't achieved: bring your awareness to what you are doing now and to how skilfully you are approaching it.

Allow yourself to enjoy the experience – and be active in searching out the fun and interest in what you are studying. See Chapter 32.

Don't stay with one study task longer than feels reasonably comfortable – alternate study tasks so that you can maintain interest and attention.

Include Metta meditations as part of your regular practice. See Chapters 21 and 23.

Don't belittle yourself if others seem to do better at their studies – people progress at different rates for different tasks, topics and skills and at different times in their lives. With time, strategy and good study habits, you can achieve well (see Cottrell, *The Study Skills Handbook*).

Don't force yourself to study – encourage and inspire yourself instead.

Be kind to your mind (see page 72).

Don't criticize yourself in a negative way if your mind wanders when studying – just return to the study task. Consider varying your study tasks to help increase the proportion of time that you spend focused 'on task', over the duration of each study session.

Don't force a particular outcome. Hold your objectives gently in mind and be open to other possible outcomes occurring. If you do your best and don't gain the objective, either try again, adapting your approach, or let yourself move on to other things.

Don't think in terms of 'right' and 'wrong' ways of studying. Consider whether your study behaviours and attitudes are 'skilled' or 'unskilled' in helping you to achieve what you wish for academically, without damaging your health, mental health, relationships with others, and your happiness.

32

Finding the joy in study

Beginner's mind

Typically, when students start a new course, although they may feel a little apprehensive about what it will be like, they bring a sense of excitement, optimism, curiosity and eagerness to get started. Their mental 'script' or messaging is a positive one.

Jaded mind

Whilst some people love everything about studying, even the most committed student can find their initial interest wanes or that it is hard to focus when reading or writing for the course. This can result from:

- Hearing others moaning about their studies
- Finding the work is harder than they anticipated
- Not doing as well as they expected
- Having to spend more time studying than planned
- Constant emphasis on grades, the course's reputation and securing a graduate job distracting them from the joy of learning.

They may feel the pressure to succeed is too great and fear failure. It can be hard to concentrate when there are high expectations, so many other distractions, or if study seems boring or too difficult.

Barriers to enjoyment

Our thoughts, feelings and emotions about study can be a help or a hindrance. They can help us engage enthusiastically or can be obstacles that prevent us from enjoying the experience and gaining the most from it.

It is worth taking a few moments now and again to touch base with how you feel, think and speak about your study, the positives and the negatives. Bring your awareness to the messages around you that nurture a sense of enjoyment and contentment with study, or a sense of dissatisfaction. You can use the following pages to becoming more aware of how your own thoughts and feelings are shaping your study experience.

Awareness of feelings towards study

Take a moment to tune in and see whether any of the following positive statements resonate with how you feel about your study. (You will get a chance to explore less positive feelings, if any, later.)

Activity: (A) Awareness of positives

1. *Underline any of the words and phrases below that echo positive feelings you have about your studies at present.*
2. *Then highlight or ⟨circle⟩ the most accurate.*

Excited! Curious! Keen to get going/ to learn more! I'm up for it!

I want to know more! I look forward to it! Great!

I think this will be good for me! I enjoy it! Interesting assignments! I welcome the mental challenge!

I love learning new things I feel passionate about this subject Enthusiastic!

It's brilliant! All good! Really useful! Stimulating!

It makes me think! It's fun! Love it!

⚑ Reflection: Tuning in to 'study positives'

1. In a typical week, how often do you respond in the ways you indicated above?
2. How easy was it to identify with positive phrases about study?
3. What would it feel like to have such phrases in your mind for a greater part of every week?
4. Which aspects of your studies do you enjoy the most?

Activity: (B) Awareness of negatives

Now, consider whether any of the comments below (or others similar to these) resonate with how you feel about your study.

~ _Underline those words and phrases below that echo any negative feelings you have about your studies at present._

~ _Then highlight or (circle) the most accurate._

I just have to get
through this in order   What if I fail?   Boring!   I can't do it!
to get a better job ...

   Too difficult!   What if I make a   Not more   Scary!
             fool of myself?   reading!

It has no
relevance   I don't read   I'm no good   It's stressing
for me!   feedback on   at this!   me out!   Dull!
     my work!

  Unfortunately, I have   I dread getting
  got an assignment to   Too much!   Hate it!   my work back
  do now.   from tutors

Back to the   I don't like this   I didn't really
grindstone!   I hate Mondays!   aspect of the   want to do this
                  course!   course!

♟ Reflection: Tuning in to 'study negatives'

1. In a typical week, how often do you respond as above to your study?
2. Are there other negative thoughts that you have about your study, your learning, your course or your capabilities?
3. What do you think are the effects of these on you and your studies?
4. Does the way you speak about your study reflect how you really feel?

👁 Mindful observation 1: Reactions to study

1. Pause every now and again to take in how you are feeling and thinking about your studies. Notice your thoughts and reactions, positive, negative and neutral, to different kinds of study task. Jot down your observations.

2. After a few days, read over your observations and reflect on these. Note whether these are more like (A) or (B) on pages 116–17 above.

👁 Mindful observation 2: The reaction of others

1. Pause occasionally to observe the kinds of comments and attitudes that other people convey about study. Are these more like (A) or (B)?

2. Which kinds of comments are you most likely to tune in to or join in?

3. What is the impact of these on you and your attitude towards study?

👁 Mindful observation 3: Communicating your reactions

1. Observe the kinds of comments you catch yourself making to others or when other people are present. Are these generally more like (A) or (B)?

2. How do other people respond? Do they reinforce your responses, or contradict them? What is the effect of this on you and on them?

3. Jot down your observations.

🔔 Reflection: Food for thought about study

All of these comments and responses are the 'food' with which you nourish your mind's attitude to study. Use your observations above to consider:

1. With what kind of messages are you 'feeding your mind' about how it can and should respond to study tasks?

2. Are these messages helping or hindering your studies? For example, do they make you want to get down to study or to find excuses for not doing it? To feel good about study or to resent it?

3. What could you change about the way you speak about study that could help you feel better about your studies?

The enjoyment in studying

There is enjoyment to be found in learning anything, if you are open to it. Experts in any topic or activity find matters of interest and enjoyment that others overlook. Once they start to look for it, people find all kinds of things to enjoy about studying. Below are just some.

Activity: What I enjoy about my studies

Consider which of these resonate with you. Highlight these.

The people in my class.

The great support I get from my friends.

Satisfaction at finding a piece of information I can use in a report.

Feelings of being more expert.

The smell of the paper in old books.

Weird facts, they make me laugh.

Just being so absorbed in a new topic.

Learning new things.

Knowing I know more.

Getting better at study!

When I suddenly 'get it'!

Knowing what I am doing.

The challenge!

Great class discussions.

Amazement at some of the things I discover.

Realizing how lucky and privileged I am to get to do this.

The quiet.

Mastering difficult bits.

Satisfaction at completing an assignment.

Seeing my report take shape as I change a little bit here and there.

The kindness of the staff.

I just like it.

Observation: The enjoyment I gain from my studies

From time to time, bring your awareness to what there is to enjoy in the study task you are undertaking. Notice your own enjoyment of the process. Observe what exactly brings you a sense of contentment, interest, well-being, fun in what you are doing. Jot these observations down. Use your insights on days when you need inspiration to study.

Generate good feelings towards study

If you feel good about your studies and your ability to learn, you will enjoy the process more. You will be less likely to resent the time you spend on it, and even look forward to your next study session.

The act of looking for things that you like or enjoy, or for which you feel grateful, triggers a chemical reaction in the brain, encouraging it to release the 'feel-good' hormone, serotonin. This can make you feel less stressed and it helps you to associate your studies with positive emotions.

Create a list

Drawing on your consideration of items on page 119 and your observations of your study, use the following page to create a 'joy list'. Jot down everything that you can think of that you:

- enjoy about study
- enjoy about your course
- are grateful for about your course, or just being able to study at all
- like about the experience of being a student, more generally.

Use your list

In future, if you are feeling at all negative about your studies, you may welcome a boost to your enthusiasm. If so:

- Come back to this section and read through your list, absorbing what it says.
- Bring your awareness back to the aspects that have brought you enjoyment.

You may not feel as much joy at that point, but you may be able to maintain a more balanced perspective and greater equanimity about your studies.

Find the joy: List

Create a list of at least 20 things you enjoy about learning, studying and being on your course. Then look for more things. Make it a long list. Then use it (see page 120).

Re-discovering the joy in learning

Children love learning new things – they are excited by what they discover, curious about the world, and ask a lot of questions! If they don't understand, they pursue the matter, following one question with another. They see intrinsic interest in what they are discovering. As we grow older, many of us lose that sense of wonder. Occasionally, it creeps up on us as a surprise, such as when we come across something totally unexpected, or when we are travelling to new places.

How mindfulness can help ...

Mindfulness is about respecting what each moment has to offer. When we bring our attention to the moment, we notice more about it, we take in things that would normally pass us by. As a result, we discover depth in things that we would otherwise treat superficially. We are better able to notice the intrinsic interest in all kinds of things we ignored or rejected as boring. We come to recognize that most things can be interesting if we bring our attention to them fully.

It is our own brain that decides whether something is of intrinsic interest and what that interest is for us. Our brain can choose to be curious about what we are studying, and become absorbed in it.

👁 Observation: Awareness of your curiosity in the topic

Before you start to study, notice whether you are bringing a curious and interested approach to the session. If not, pause and tune in to what you are about to study. What are you likely to find out? How might you be able to use that information? Are you open to finding things interesting, useful, awe-inspiring, life changing?

Whilst you are studying, become aware of whether you have drifted from that state of mind. If so, pause and tune in to it again. When you have finished a study session, take a few moments to consider what you have discovered. Value what you have learnt. Value the opportunity that you have had to learn.

33

Want it? Hate it? Lost the plot?

Three dominant thought patterns …

The more we practise mindfulness, the more we become aware of the thoughts and feelings that arise. Without dwelling on these, we become aware of those which recur or have special strength. We start to notice the power these exert over our habitual ways of thinking, our responses to the world, our actions and behaviours, whether helpfully or unhelpfully.

Traditional practice in mindfulness draws attention to three kinds of thought pattern that drive much of our behaviour and affect our happiness.

1. 'Cravings' or 'wants'

Craving is about wanting things in such a way that there is a good chance they are distracting, and/or lead to a sense of disappointment, anti-climax, failure or loss. Cravings may be excessive attachment to goals, to things you want to do, be, gain or achieve.

I want 100% for all my work

Oh no! Not a 9 a.m. lecture!

2. 'Aversions' or 'don't wants'.

These may be feelings of hate, dislike, boredom, annoyance, irritation, or similar. We turn away from, avoid, or don't engage adequately with, things we don't like.

3. 'Delusions'

These include misunderstandings, fooling ourselves, fanciful thinking and mistaken beliefs. They arise from not letting ourselves be fully aware of how things are. Cravings and aversions can give rise to delusions. For example, we delude ourselves when we believe we 'really need' something, when in reality we want rather than need it.

I must have chocolate to complete this report!!!

Reinforcing thought patterns ...

Cravings, aversions and delusions reinforce each other. That can make our typical responses seem very powerful, logical and irresistible, even when based on weak foundations. For example:

- If we have strong desires for things we do not possess, we might delude ourselves about their relative significance, and feel bad about ourselves for failing to gain them. These could be a desire to get the best mark or a particular grade, a place on the sports team, gaining a prize, or being allocated to the study group we wanted.

- If we don't feel happy about our study outcomes, we might convince ourselves that other people or circumstances, or even our books, are to blame, and develop an aversion towards these. That aversion is based on a delusion.

- If we crave material objects or particular kinds of success or celebrity in order to fill emotional gaps, we are deluding ourselves that these would address the underlying unhappiness, loss or sense of failure. If we don't get what we need, we might feel aversion towards our circumstances, other people, or ourselves, as an excuse not to deal with the emotional gap.

- Cravings for a particular result can drive us to study or work excessively, deluding ourselves that this is helpful and making us averse to advice about balance, breaks, sleep, food and exercise.

Attachment to cravings, aversions and delusion

We tend to form strong attachments to our cravings, aversions and delusions. They become familiar – like an old coat or pair of shoes. Although they might constrain our actions or pinch our toes, we don't want to throw them away.

Part of our identity?

These thought patterns can feel like a core part of who we are, woven into what we think is our identity. We may be reluctant to give them up, or to release their hold on us, in case we don't recognize who we then become. That can feel rather scary.

Rather too useful ...?

Our aversions provide great excuses for not attending that lecture, not researching that topic, not reading that book, not getting down to study, not contributing to that group. It can be handy to have someone or something else to blame so we can avoid acknowledging that we could look at everything with completely different eyes.

The impact of cravings, aversions and delusions on study

Typically, these thought patterns lead to students losing out. They make study less effective and detract from its enjoyment. They divert students' attention, so that they are not engaged fully in thoughts and activities that best help them get to grips with their courses. They waste energies and valuable study time, so that students don't gain all the knowledge, understanding and skill that they could have done otherwise. As a result, however well the students do, they have not gained fully from the opportunity of being a student, and not achieved their potential.

Sometimes, such thought patterns are more serious in their effects. They feed stress or get in the way of acknowledging existing feelings of anxiety. They can bolster self-harming behaviours that undermine students' security, health and sense of well-being. Sometimes, they are used to justify cheating in order to achieve a better result, or to defend not studying at all.

Curiously, these thought patterns can lead students to avoid the study for which they have signed up, and which usually cost them a great deal. They are employed to encourage collusion in negative thinking that drains the excitement and interest from study, encouraging procrastination and ineffective study habits.

The power of cravings, aversions and delusions

Cravings, aversions and delusions creep back and poke at us, over and over. They weave their way into our day, usually without us really noticing that they are …

Distracting us from our focus

  Stealing our attention

    Absorbing our energies

      Derailing us from our best intentions

        Leaving us feeling unsatisfied, discontented or miserable.

34

Managing study aversions

It is important that you don't let your study aversions take over and rule your studies. Usually, that means doing a number of things.

1. Be aware of your aversions.
2. Recognize that your aversions do not have to be fixed: you can change how you think and feel about any aspect of your study.
3. Observe the way your study aversions affect you and your studies, so you are clear about their impact.
4. Through greater self-awareness, become better at catching the moment when aversions start to form.
5. Re-shape the way you think about study tasks, and how you go about them, so that you respond differently when you recognize that an aversion is forming.
6. Change your study behaviours so they work better for you – so that your aversions don't get in the way of your success and enjoyment.

Recognizing your study aversions

The first step is to recognize your own pet aversions. The following activity helps you to start identifying these.

Typical aversions when studying

Below are some typical aversions associated with study, which can undermine students' potential. Identify ☑ any that ring true for you.

- [ ] I don't like studying anything I find boring
- [ ] I don't like attending so many classes
- [ ] I don't like putting time into organizing my notes, files and folders
- [ ] I don't like studying on my own
- [ ] I don't want to work in groups with people I haven't chosen
- [ ] I don't like doing presentations or speaking in front of others
- [ ] I don't want to do all that reading
- [ ] I hate all the 'big words'
- [ ] I don't like writing essays
- [ ] I don't want feedback that tells me what I have done wrong
- [ ] I hate tests and exams

Note down any others that you can think of that apply to you.

(1) ....

(2) ....

(3) ....

(4) ....

(5) ....

Signs of study aversion

Once you become aware that you are acting on your aversions, you can pause and consider how to respond more skilfully so that these have less effect. It is useful if you can notice as early as possible the signs that you are reacting to a study aversion. You may recognize some of those below.

Signs of study aversions: Things to watch out for

Which of these signs of study aversion do you recognize in yourself?

- [ ] Obsessing about things I don't like
- [ ] Procrastinating: putting off certain study tasks
- [ ] Taking a long time to settle into the task
- [ ] Giving up easily once started
- [ ] Interrupting study tasks unnecessarily after a short time
- [ ] Getting bored
- [ ] Not turning up to class
- [ ] Spending time thinking about how I 'can't do it'
- [ ] Moaning, complaining or grumbling about some aspect of study
- [ ] Feeling anxiety building
- [ ] Letting my attention wander
- [ ] Pausing for food or drink when I don't really need them
- [ ] Fidgeting, clicking pens, tapping my feet, etc.
- [ ] Completing a task without really knowing what I learnt

Reflection: Signs of study aversion

- ~ Consider whether there are other signs in your study behaviour that suggest that you are not engaging fully with your studies.
- ~ How good are you at recognizing early signs of study aversion?

Observation: Becoming more aware of study aversions

Over the next few days, if you catch yourself feeling negative about any aspect of study, bring your attention to that. Jot down your observations to help you become more mindful of the impact of such aversions on you and your study. The prompts below may help you to consider your potential study aversions.

Prompts

1. Which aspects of your study are prompting the most negative thoughts and reactions at the moment?
2. What gives rise to these study aversions?
3. How do you respond when you notice them? Are they easy to spot straight away? Do you give in to them easily, or at all?
4. How do these aversions affect the way you approach study tasks? For example, do you put off study?
5. Do they affect you in other ways – such as how you think about yourself? Your course? Other people?
6. Are you able to get past your study aversions when you need to? What helps you to do this?
7. Do you need help in coping with them or are they relatively easy to manage?

Reflection: Taking charge of study aversions

Read through your observations about your study aversions.

~ Consider how you might approach those aspects of your study differently.

~ What would you need to do, say, or think to help that along?

~ How could you draw on mindfulness and Metta practice to help?

35

Wanting, craving, grasping

Wanting things – a lot!

It can be relatively easy to recognize that aversions, the things we try to avoid or don't like, have a negative effect. We can observe how they affect study, life, work, well-being. It may be more surprising to recognize that wanting too much, or 'craving', can have similar negative effects.

This doesn't mean that it is wrong to want things – that can motivate you to overcome great obstacles, build character, do social good and inspire others. On the other hand, grasping after particular outcomes can be unhelpful, depending on why you want things so much and what the effect of this is on you and others. It is a question of:

- ～ what you want and why
- ～ what you have to do to get it
- ～ how much you want it and how you will feel if you don't get it
- ～ who or what might benefit or get damaged along the way
- ～ how you will feel if you do get what you want – whether it will really bring you contentment.

Enjoy your aspirations

You can have high aspirations for your study whilst still being mindful. It is natural to want to achieve well as a student, to gain a good job, to be happy and healthy, to lead a good life. Low aspirations can be compatible with mindfulness, too – it depends why you want to achieve little in terms of your study.

However, many students have low aspirations for reasons such as poor self-esteem, previous bad educational results, or doubt in their ability. As a result, they don't engage with their learning in ways that could bring them enjoyment, interest, well-being, contentment and achievement.

The important thing is to be conscious of the choices you make: to be clear of what you are doing, how and why. Become more aware of how you feel about the choices you are making. Nobody else can do these things for you.

🧘 Reflection: Personal aspirations

~ What are your aspirations for your time as a student – what do you want to gain from this experience, and to bring to it?

~ Do you think these aspirations are too high, too low, or just right?

~ What lies behind these aspirations: why are they important to you?

~ Given the aspirations you have set, do you follow through in doing the things necessary to achieve them? If not, why not?

Grasping too much for good grades?

Typically, gaining a qualification is a costly and time-consuming process. It involves sacrifices of time, money, energy, family and social life. Students can put too much pressure on themselves to get good grades, falling into unhelpful thought patterns and behaviours. These include:

~ Neglecting important aspects of study, such as nurturing interest and curiosity in their subjects, finding pleasure in discovering new things, developing their understanding, and enjoying the process

~ Neglecting family, friends, health, and relationships

~ Experiencing anxiety, excess stress, powerlessness or desperation

~ Thinking about cheating and plagiarizing – or even doing so

~ Self-harming, alcohol, substance abuse or chronic neglect of sleep, rest, exercise, and/or nutrition.

However essential you might feel it is to gain great grades, it is just as important to keep high aspirations in perspective.

🧘 Reflection: Mindful aspirations

~ Is your attitude towards your grades helpful: does it prompt sufficient effort? Or too much?

~ How do your aspirations affect the way you think about your study – do they help you enjoy it or reduce your sense of happiness?

~ Do they lead you to grasp too much after good grades?

~ Do they induce unskilful thought patterns and behaviours?

Cravings for 'quick fixes'

When the finishing line for gaining a qualification seems a long way off, it can be tempting to search for 'quick' fixes to fill in the gaps created by the sacrifices you are making. Usually these take the form of finding distractions from a sense of discontent, such as through checking social media, seeking out entertainment, or eating junk food. It may involve looking for ways of reducing the workload, such as not attending class, not preparing for class, not doing as much reading as is desirable, or looking for short-cuts to completing assignments.

'Rewards for study' versus 'intrinsic motivation'

Another form of 'craving' is needing a 'reward' for what you do. When it is difficult to get down to study, it can be very helpful to devise a system of rewards to boost your motivation. It can also be a good way of managing time so that you don't put off study until you have had all your treats and indulged all your habits for getting distracted.

However, it is even better to develop the skill of concentrating mindfully on what you have to do without needing to set motivational rewards. You can bring your awareness to finding purpose and interest in what you do, so that the motivation is within yourself – or 'intrinsic' to you. This has many benefits:

- If you can find the enjoyment in the task, that is 'reward' in itself
- It liberates you from needing rewards in order to do things
- It brings greater contentment and less stress
- You learn more if you are fully present in the task, taking in what you are discovering and thinking about it, rather than if you 'go through the motions' to some extent in order to gain a separate reward.

Bringing awareness to your 'wants'

If you find that the route towards achieving what you think you want actually leaves you feeling bad about yourself, or anxious, miserable, angry, hostile, ill or disappointed, then it is worth bringing your awareness to why that is so. You may decide that the eventual goal is worth the downsides. You may find there are ways to bring more enjoyment, or at least less unhappiness, to the process of getting to where you want to be.

Typical cravings when studying

Below are some typical cravings associated with student life and study. Identify ☑ any that ring true for you.

- [ ] Wanting to check messages, texts, emails, social media, etc.
- [ ] Wanting to buy junk food
- [ ] Wanting to get good grades – at all costs
- [ ] Craving alcohol or other mind-altering substances
- [ ] Wanting (often) to continue with activities that go on late into the night, even though there is study or work the next day
- [ ] Wanting to do anything else except study
- [ ] Wanting to chat about an irrelevant aspect of study, the course, the people on it, rather than actually studying
- [ ] Suddenly needing to do other things such as eat, sleep, drink, grumble, complain, smoke, exercise, talk to friends during study time
- [ ] Craving to be in a future time when the course is over

If these particular examples don't apply to you, jot down any that do.

👁 Observation: Awareness of study-related cravings

During the week, take note of feelings of wanting or needing things urgently or with intensity. When do these cravings occur? What things do you crave? Do you really need these? How do you respond? How do they affect your use of study time?

Are you able to settle into study and stick with it without the need for rewards?

Jot down your observations to help you become more aware of the impact of such cravings.

36

Self-delusional thinking about study

Self-delusion obstructs our perspective. Nonetheless, most of us are fond of resorting to this as part of our thinking repertoire. We can be quite good at fooling ourselves, not being aware of this until much later. It diverts us nicely at moments when we don't want to face up to what we need to do.

'Delusion' is a strong word. We don't generally like to think of ourselves as being 'deluded'. However, we are pretty good at being like ostriches, sticking our head in the sand to avoid seeing exactly how things are and how we contribute to situations through what we do and don't do.

Deluding ourselves about study

It is to be expected that we will engage in mistaken beliefs and inaccurate thinking about our study, and about ourselves as students, just as we do about other parts of our lives.

When studying, this can mean such things as persuading ourselves that we are busy on a task when we are not, that all is fine when it isn't, that we deserve things that we haven't really earned, that we are achieving the right study/life balance. Lecturers and tutors encounter a huge number of self-delusions about study every year – and as you might expect, the same kinds of thinking come up again and again. You are probably all too aware of some of these in yourself and other students.

Tackling self-delusion

Delusive thinking can make us feel better in the moment but it doesn't address the underlying issues. We are fooling ourselves until we:

~ recognize self-delusion in our thoughts and actions

~ understand why we are deluding ourselves and recognize a different way of doing things

~ change our thinking and actions accordingly.

As a starting place, look through some examples of self-deluding thought patterns that are typical of student life. These illustrate how easy it is to slip into such ways of thinking, and the many ways of doing so.

Recognizing self-deluding thinking

~ *Look through the following examples of mistaken or self-deluding thinking. These are not uncommon.*

~ *Consider honestly which of these, if any, apply to you. Check ☑ those that do.*

☐ Persuading myself I am studying when I am mainly getting distracted

☐ Thinking that I can do well without putting in the hours

☐ Convincing myself that I will feel more like studying next week than I do today

☐ Reacting to study as if classes, assignments, coursework, exams, or student life and opportunities will go on forever

☐ Believing that other students don't experience similar difficulties and challenges to mine

☐ Believing other students are naturally more clever or talented (rather than considering that they may have put in many more relevant study hours, either recently or over their lifetime)

☐ Believing I am smarter than other people

☐ Convincing myself that if something is 'boring' then I don't need to consider it

☐ Assuming that I don't really need to read course handbooks

☐ Telling myself that I don't need to find out about the regulations that affect my course of study

☐ Acting as if 'peeping' isn't cheating when I am testing my recall of information

☐ Convincing myself that throwing last minute 'all-nighters' is a good idea

☐ Believing that grades I receive result mainly from good or bad luck

- [ ] Believing there is little I can do to improve my grades
- [ ] Persuading myself that there is little I can do to improve the standard of my work
- [ ] Telling myself that it won't be helpful to set myself a practice exam before I sit an exam
- [ ] Thinking that I have to study non-stop in order to do well
- [ ] Believing that my assignment deserves good marks because I made an effort (even though I missed the point about what was required)
- [ ] Thinking I should pass my exams (even though I didn't start to study for these until the last minute, or didn't revise well)
- [ ] Convincing myself I can miss classes without losing out
- [ ] Believing that as I learnt grammar and punctuation when I was at school, I don't need to check whether my use of language is as good as I think it is
- [ ] Persuading myself that I don't need to adapt my everyday communication to meet the different requirements of academic work
- [ ] Convincing myself that it is a good idea to copy more or less word for word from the books
- [ ] Telling myself it is fine to 'cut and paste' from electronic sources into my notes or assignments
- [ ] Telling myself that it is OK to purchase essays and assignments online or from others
- [ ] Convincing myself that my citations and references are fine, even though I haven't checked these are correct in all details

Other ways? What other ways do you try to persuade yourself of things about study when you know you are being over-optimistic, 'hoping for the best' or just want things to be different?

🛕 Reflection: Recognizing self-delusions about study

- ↝ Of the items that you have checked ☑ as relevant to you, which ones have the most effect on your action and study?
- ↝ What are the consequences of such thinking?

Why we try to delude ourselves ...

On the surface, it may appear a strange thing to do, to delude ourselves about reality. However, we do so because we believe we will benefit from it in some way. Not facing up to things as they really are serves a range of purposes, such as these below.

1. It can help us cope emotionally with difficult situations, through persuading ourselves things are not as bad as they seem.

2. It helps us to avoid painful thoughts and feelings, such as by denying we have these or pretending they don't matter.

3. It helps us to believe we are right, which feels more comfortable even when we have a sense that we are not.

4. It provides excuses for doing or getting what we want (giving in to cravings).

5. It provides excuses for not doing, or facing up to, what we don't like (giving in to aversions).

6. It helps us to put off, or avoid, things that we don't want to do, even when we know these are the right thing to do.

7. It enables us to justify our behaviour, when it may be uncomfortable to face up to what we have done.

Reflection: Reasons for deluding yourself

~ Do you recognize any of the reasons above as true of you?

~ When are you most likely to use some, or all, of the above?

Understanding self-deluding study behaviours

Below, you will find some examples of self-deluding thought patterns and behaviours. These are typical psychological ploys, or 'defence mechanisms', that we use to avoid aspects of reality.

- Consider the examples given and whether these are true of you.
- Add, and consider, your own personal examples.

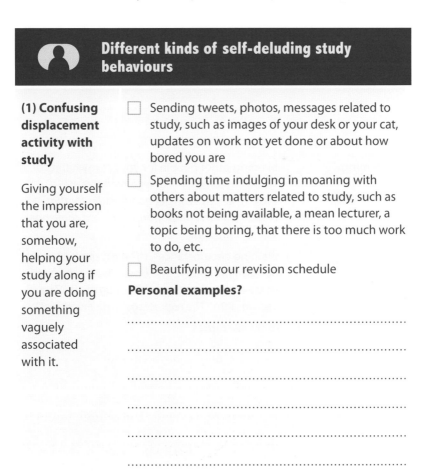

Different kinds of self-deluding study behaviours

(1) Confusing displacement activity with study

Giving yourself the impression that you are, somehow, helping your study along if you are doing something vaguely associated with it.

☐ Sending tweets, photos, messages related to study, such as images of your desk or your cat, updates on work not yet done or about how bored you are

☐ Spending time indulging in moaning with others about matters related to study, such as books not being available, a mean lecturer, a topic being boring, that there is too much work to do, etc.

☐ Beautifying your revision schedule

Personal examples?

....

....

....

....

....

....

(2) Denial

Pretending there isn't a problem or issue to address when there is.

☐ Denying that you haven't as much time for an assignment as you want to believe. (*'I haven't done those tasks for my assignment yet but there is loads of time' – when there isn't.*)

☐ Pretending it doesn't matter that there are fundamental gaps or flaws in your assignment. (*'My essay doesn't really address the title, but it will be OK.' 'My assignment was great. I don't know why it didn't get a better mark.'*)

Personal examples

....

....

....

....

(3) Blaming

Attributing to others the responsibility for things that go wrong, rather than recognizing your own role.

☐ Blaming other people for your study habits or study outcomes. (*'That lecturer hates me – there is no way I can get good grades for that class.' 'I was in a weak group – I lacked challenge.' 'I got no support.'*)

☐ Blaming circumstances. (*'There weren't enough books in the library.' 'The classes were scheduled at the wrong time for me.' 'The dog ate it!' 'The bus was late.' 'The technology wasn't working!'*)

Personal examples

....

....

....

....

(4) Excuses and rationalisations

Finding excuses to justify unskilful thinking and action

☐ Reasoning with ourselves about why we are really doing something when we know we are looking for excuses. (*'It would be better to watch the film now and study through the night when it is quieter', 'It doesn't matter if I do other things during class time'.*)

Personal examples

....

....

....

....

....

....

....

....

....

Observation: Awareness of self-deluding behaviours

~ Set yourself the task of pausing and taking note when you catch yourself trying to persuade or convince yourself in self-deluding ways.

~ At such times, acknowledge the self-deluding thought.

~ Put a little time between the thought and any follow-up behaviour.

~ Pause to consider the consequences for you and others.

~ Then decide whether to continue or to change your course of action.

37

Building your powers of attention

The value of attention

Good attentional capability brings a range of benefits to study:

- **Greater contentment:** Absorption in what you are doing brings a greater sense of task satisfaction even when the task might not at first seem particularly fun or entertaining.

- **Improved focus:** The ability to apply your mind fully to complex problems and other tasks that require sustained focus, so you continue to take in the information that you need.

- **More efficient thought-processing**, so that you can follow a complex set of ideas through to their logical conclusion, or follow directions, instructions and formulae in a logical, sustained way.

- **Improved memory function**, such as better retention and recall of material that you hear, read or revise.

- **More effective use of time:** You waste less time through mind-wandering, task-switching, losing your place, re-doing activities or filling in gaps caused by losses in attention.

How mindfulness can help

Mindfulness is not about forcing your attention, or gritting your teeth to maintain concentration. It is about becoming better at:

- Directing and maintaining your focus
- Being better at noticing when your attention has wandered from your focus and that you are distracted
- Being able to acknowledge what distracted you, without getting caught up in that thought stream
- Gently directing attention back to the original focus, without judging.

What does research tell us about mindfulness and attention?

There is a vast, and growing, amount of research into the beneficial effects of mindfulness on attentional processes. Here are two examples.

Improved attention and recall

In an experiment conducted by the University of Washington, different groups were provided with an eight-week training course in either meditation or relaxation techniques. After eight weeks, participants who had engaged in daily mindfulness practice reported greater awareness and attention than the groups that didn't receive mindfulness training (Levy et al., 2012). In addition, it was found that they had improved their memory of the details of the tasks they were undertaking. The researchers attributed this improved memory to the effect of reduced stress, brought about by mindfulness practice (see page 151 below).

Maintaining alertness

In the USA, there was interest in how to train militia prior to their deployment, in order to help them remain alert to their general situation following time spent in demanding, high-attention tasks. This was important as militia were especially prone at such times to letting their attention slip, making them less able to spot potential danger and risks to themselves and others. Groups of trainees were provided with different kinds of training, or with no training. It was found that the military trainees who received eight weeks of training and practice in mindfulness were better than all the other groups at maintaining their attention at the required times (Jha et al., 2015).

Different aspects of attention

Attention itself consists of different aspects. Research by Good (Good et al., 2015) found that mindfulness practice has a positive effect on three key aspects: stability, control, and efficiency. These are explored below.

1. Attentional stability

We learn new skills best when we immerse ourselves fully in difficult and complex tasks. If tasks consist of too little challenge, our brains learn to perform them on auto-pilot. This automatic function has advantages for us as humans as it means we can perform some complex tasks such as breathing, balancing, thinking and walking at the same time.

The downside is that our brains switch onto auto-pilot when we are learning and need to be paying attention. It has been estimated that for most of us, our minds wander for around 50% of the time. You experience this at times when you get to the end of a page when reading but can't recall anything you read.

Mindfulness practice trains your mind to attend to what is in front of it and to catch, early on, when the mind moves onto something else. Research shows that mindfulness helps us to stabilize our attention on what we are doing (Smallwood and Schooler, 2015). For those who have meditated for a long time, this can be observed in the neural activity of their brains (Brewer et al., 2011; Pagnoni, 2012). Sometimes, we get great ideas when our minds wander but, for most study tasks, such as listening, reading, writing and debating, it is helpful if we can maintain our focus through stable attention.

2. Attentional control

When we are studying, it is easy to get distracted by interesting links on the internet, messages coming in on social media and events happening around us, as well as our own thoughts. Distractions, by definition, interrupt our focus. This wastes time. It leads to us missing essential information, forgetting great ideas, and losing our place or our 'flow' in the task. Weak attentional control affects study efficiency and effectiveness.

Those who meditate are better at focusing their attention without getting distracted, even in more difficult situations such as when emotional matters are involved (Tang et al., 2007; Allen et al., 2012). This is supported by neurological research into brain wave activity, which shows that experienced meditators are better at identifying distractions when these arise and at disengaging from them (Cahn, Delorme, and Polich, 2013).

3. Attentional efficiency

Our attentional capacity is limited. If we have to make an effort to avoid distraction, then we are using up that limited resource, leaving fewer resources for other things we need to attend to.

Mindfulness practice, by improving stability and control, also makes us more efficient in the way we use our attentional resources so that we use fewer of these to manage distractions (Cahn and Polich, 2009; Slagter et al., 2007). This is reported by meditators themselves (Tang et al., 2015) and is also indicated by fMRI scans of their brains (Kozasa et al., 2012; Lutz et al., 2009).

This research suggests that mindfulness practice can be useful to students. It helps them to manage distractions and mind-wandering so that they can concentrate better, whether in class or when studying on their own.

38

Multi-tasking – and being 'fully present'

Many people pride themselves on their multi-tasking abilities, yet research indicates that the brain can only focus on one thing at a time (Miller, 2016). The sensation of multi-tasking on complex tasks is just an illusion. This may seem strange, since many people think they are multi-tasking efficiently all the time. The illusion arises from the brain flitting back and forth quickly between tasks, or 'task-switching', without us being aware of this.

Slower brain

Having several tasks on the go doesn't mean that the brain is working well. Instead, this puts the brain into a continual state of only partially paying attention to anything. As the brain can only focus on one thing, it just slows down.

Stressed brain ...

If it is constantly multi-tasking, the brain becomes over-worked, inefficient and stressed. Such activity can keep the 'fight or flight' response continually activated, releasing stress hormones such as cortisol, which is not good for our bodies in the long term (Stone, 2009).

Ineffective brain

Multi-tasking means we don't use our brain in the way it needs us to in order to function at its best. Our brains need spaces and pauses in order to form strong neural connections in particular regions of the brain; this is necessary so that it can absorb and recall material, as well as for things such as tuning in to empathy for others, creativity, and feelings of compassion.

What does research tell us about multi-tasking?

1. Focusing on one task at a time is better for study

Students who engage in *less* multi-tasking are better motivated for independent study, and better able to stay focused on their work. Splitting attention between tasks leads to superficial 'rote' learning whereas focusing on one task makes it easier to transfer learning to new contexts (Foerde et al., 2006). Dividing attention between tasks is linked to negative emotional responses to study and less efficient study (Willingham, 2010; Calderwell et al., 2014). As mindfulness is about being fully present on the task in hand, it fosters more efficient study.

2. Switching task can be useful after some focused study

When you have focused on a piece of work for a while, it can be beneficial to put it aside so that the brain can absorb the material and incubate ideas. Returning later, refreshed, can help bring energy and renewed interest; the brain may even come up with solutions to problems during that 'down' period.

Aha! Now I understand what that chapter was about!

3. Everyday task-switching has bad effects on study

Everyday multi-tasking such as using technology in class or at home has a negative effect on studying, on learning during lectures, reading, and on marks or grades (Carrier et al., 2015).

4. 'Multi-tasking' with multiple media increases distractibility

Levine et al. (2012) found that higher use of mobile media is associated with greater distractibility and impulsiveness, with poor consequences for learning and for efficient thinking. A further study, by Rosen et al. (2013a), observed students studying minute by minute for over 15 minutes. Students struggled to maintain their attention on their main task for more than 6 minutes at a time, and wasted about a third of their time doing things such as walking around, texting, using social media and watching TV. The greater number of distracting devices students have open at the start of study, the less likely they are to stay on task.

5. Belief in being a 'gifted multi-tasker' is misguided

Ophir and other researchers at Stanford University (2009) found that students who think they are gifted multi-taskers perform worse than those who prefer to do one task at a time. The high-level multi-taskers were weak at filtering out irrelevant distractions. They were also weaker at switching between tasks and at organizing their thoughts. This is a good example of craving (for distraction through multi-tasking) feeding a delusion (that they are good at it).

Persistent multi-taskers believed that they could switch to being 'laser-focused' if needed. It was found that they had developed deeply inefficient thinking habits that prevented this. Even when they stopped multi-tasking, they were still easily distracted from what they were doing.

6. It can take 15–25 minutes to become deeply absorbed

When you switch task, the brain has a great deal more work to do. After every switch in task, it has to refocus attention, work out what is needed, then work out where it had got to previously with the first task, as well as pick up again on the various ideas and thoughts you had had. It can take 15–25 minutes to become fully absorbed again (Mark et al., 2008).

7. Switching tasks can reduce study efficiency by 40%

Students solving maths problems took 40% longer when they were required to switch task (Buetti and Lleras, 2016). Other studies suggest that multi-taskers can still work fast, with greater effort, but then feel negative and pressurized (Mark et al., 2008).

8. The negative impact on the brain could be long-term

Neuroscientists at the University of Sussex used MRI scans to look at the longer-term effects of multi-tasking. They found that persistent use of multiple devices was associated with reduced brain density in the anterior cingulate cortex. This suggested there could be longer-term damage to regions of the brain responsible for empathy and cognitive and emotional control (Loh and Kanai, 2014).

9. People are likely to multi-task in order to feel better

Studies indicate that students tend to switch task when they feel they are making poor progress or won't complete the current task (Adler and Benbunan-Fich, 2013). Changing task makes it more likely that you don't then complete what you do.

10. 'Multi-taskers' aren't aware of the effects ...

Those who switch tasks a lot are not aware that they have missed information. They tend to be oblivious to the effect of their distracted multi-tasking on themselves and on people around them. This behaviour can come across as rude, inconvenient and time-wasting to other people.

⚓ Reflection: Multi-tasking and task-switching

Consider the above research into multi-tasking and task-switching.

~ Which findings have some relevance for you?

~ Do you consider yourself to be a skilled multi-tasker? If so, how might you be losing out in terms of actual attention to study?

~ Which aspects of your study are most likely to be affected by the way you engage in 'task-switching'?

What is the net effect of multi-tasking and task-switching on study?

As the research above indicates, because the brain can only focus on one thing at a time, multi-tasking leads to disorganized thinking, missed information, inefficient working, and poorer quality work, resulting in poorer grades. For persistent multi-taskers, many common study tasks that require sustained attention are likely to be a challenge. These include:

~ Remaining engaged for the length of a typical lecture or seminar

~ Maintaining attention long enough to absorb what is really important when listening in lectures and seminars

~ Reading for sustained periods with attention and good recall

~ Sticking with a research task online without getting distracted

~ Completing study tasks in the most efficient sequence

~ Being aware when they have missed information, and so realizing that they need to make that up later

~ Following through on complex ideas that require the sustained application of critical thought or problem-solving

~ Remaining fully focused for the duration of an exam.

All is not lost ...!

The good news is that the brain is malleable – you can create different kinds of neural networks even in adulthood, depending on what you do. If you reduce your task-switching, you can train your brain to develop better attention.

How mindfulness can help

In the experiment conducted by Levy et al. (2012) mentioned on page 144, those who received the meditation training were not only better at staying on task, they also made fewer 'task switches'. The reduced task-switching seems to arise as a consequence of mindful activity, as participants hadn't been asked explicitly not to engage in 'multi-tasking'.

Things you can do ...

1. Be aware of the negative impact of task-switching or 'multi-tasking' on your study – and on your brain in general.
2. Become more aware of how often you are engaged in multi-tasking, and task-switching.
3. Make a conscious effort to remain focused on each task in turn and for longer. Find the intrinsic interest in what you are doing (see page 133) as this is likely to reduce your task-switching naturally.
4. Where feasible, reduce the number of technological devices around you when studying.
5. Reduce the amount of time that you spend moving between different technologies and devices.
6. Be mindful of when in the day you check messages, emails and alerts. Put aside set periods for this and focus on them for that time. For example, decide on a maximum of three or four short periods a day to check social media and messages, and one longer period if needed.
7. Use software that blocks interruptions for other times, especially when you are studying.
8. Use mindfulness meditations or activities just before studying, to help with concentration.
9. Be more aware of anyone who is waiting for you to bring your attention back to the conversation or task, if you get caught up in multi-tasking.

Reflection: Addressing multi-tasking and task-switching

1. Which of the actions above would be useful for you to adopt?
2. Are there other things you could do to improve your attention to study?
3. What could you start doing differently from today?

Observation: Gaining and regaining concentration

During the next few weeks, take notice of how long it takes you to become immersed in study tasks such as reading or writing. How long does it take you to become immersed again once you break concentration?

39

Listening mindfully in class

Why bother with classes?

Class-based study, whether in a lecture, seminar, tutorial, workshop, labs, online class, video conference or similar, is an important component of many courses. It provides a useful opportunity for you to:

1. Learn new things and gain an overview of the topic

2. Gain a sense of how your professors conceptualize topics, which is useful for your assignments, exams, and for directing your own study

3. Gain reassurance that your independent study and reading is on track – or else to gain a steer on how to adapt what you are doing

4. Take part in in-class activities and discussions, if provided

5. Pick up on useful extra material, tips, news and reminders

6. Meet up with people before and after class, staying connected with the course – and building a sense of belonging.

Listening – rather than just being in the room

Apart from being a sign of respect, listening with attention means that you learn more. Research on student attention during class shows it can be difficult to listen well even when you set out to do so, and even more so when your attention is split (see Chapter 38).

▲ Reflection: Paying attention in class

Take just a moment in class to observe how many students are really listening attentively.

➣ How many seem to be focused on what is being said rather than noting everything down?

➣ What other things do students seem to be doing other than listening and note making?

Attention in class: What does research tell us?

Wandering minds

Research shows that students' memory for lecture material is impaired by 'mind-wandering' (Lindquist and McLean, 2011; Farley et al., 2013). It makes sense to help the mind not to wander, and to find ways of improving listening, understanding and recall of what is said during class.

> ### 🔔 Reflection: Effective study during class
>
> Read through the research findings below and consider:
> - Which surprise you?
> - Which of these effects had you already noticed yourself?
> - What might these findings mean for your own study?

Using technology in class is less efficient for recall

The research about the impact of using technologies during class has mixed findings: some studies find that texting in class has the worst effect on study; others find that true mainly of Facebook. However, the combined effect of using technologies in class is negative for study. Students who used technologies, including laptops, during lectures had poorer memory scores than those who used paper and pencil (Wood et al., 2012).

Students who understand least reduce their listening

You might imagine that if you are in a lecture and are struggling to make sense of what is being said, you would increase your focus. Adler and Benbunan-Fich (2013) found that this isn't the case. Instead, when students realize that they are falling behind, they distract themselves by checking messages and texts – and miss even more.

Using laptops in class is distracting

There are advantages to using laptops in class: you can take notes in electronic form and access material relevant to the class. However, research shows that the overall effect on study isn't good. It involves a lot of task-switching, or 'multi-tasking', which isn't good for study (see Chapter 38). It affects what you take in and recall from the lecture (Wood et al., 2012).

Using technology in class reduces grades

Studies indicate that high levels of multi-tasking when using technology in class are strongly associated with poor academic results. Texting, in particular, is a key contributor to low grades (Burak, 2012; Clayson and Haley, 2012). Some studies found that students who use Facebook in class gained the lowest grades (Rosen et al., 2013a).

Sitting next to someone with a laptop is distracting

It has been found that students who used laptops in class scored lower on a test, given later, than those who didn't. However, those who were in direct view of another student using a laptop also scored lower than those who were not. Just being near a laptop user creates a significant distraction (Sana et al., 2013).

Observation: Listening attentively in class

From time to time, observe how much of the time you had lost focus in class. Bring your awareness to such things as:

~ How good is your capacity to pay attention in class? What distracts you? How can you gain a realistic sense of how much you miss?

~ How well do you prepare in advance, in order to improve your focus in class?

~ Do you make notes in such a way that you can attend to what is said – or are you so busy making notes that you miss chunks of the class?

~ Can you recall most of what was said during the class? Could you repeat the details to someone else without looking at your notes?

Things you can do

In advance of class. Check the information that you already have available to you on the topic in your books, online, or in course resource materials and handbooks. You can then feel free to listen mindfully without taking copious notes.

Choose your seat carefully. Avoid sitting next to someone using a laptop or device or who will distract you.

Listen with attention. During the lecture or class, focus on listening. Keep your technology switched off unless needed for classwork.

Just before class. Focus your attention by bringing your awareness to your breath for a minute or two, as you do in meditation. Even 15 seconds can help. You could do this when people are coming in or when waiting for the lecture to start.

Absorb as much as you can. If you start to lose track of what the lecturer is saying, don't get discouraged. Instead, listen even more attentively. Aim to capture as much as you can, listening for clues to help you to follow up on missed information later.

Make minimal notes. Just note information you can't get from books or the internet, as well as brief reminders of ideas that arise.

Paper. When writing notes, consider using paper rather than your laptop or device, to help recall later and give you more flexibility.

If you are using a laptop, device or phone in class ...

1. **Before class.** Reduce tempting distractions, closing down extra windows, sites, pages, etc.
2. **During class.** Stay focused on listening and on taking part in activities.
3. **Be strategic** – about which technology to use and when, so that you keep task-switching to a minimum.
4. **Be selective.** Avoid 'touch typing' everything that is said.
5. **Don't check mail, texts, messages.** If you can't resist, wait until the lecturer has completed a section rather than doing it when they are still speaking.
6. **Be aware of other people.** Using technology in class distracts others.

40

Using study time mindfully

Study time has its own special character

Student time doesn't seem to follow normal rules – it is like a great trickster. There may be no taught sessions scheduled for some days or weeks, so it may feel as if the course is not very demanding, with lots of free time. Suddenly, there are several assignments to submit at around the same time, exams to prepare for, work to be done for class, decisions to be made about what you are doing the following year, placements to organize, your CV to develop. There doesn't seem enough time for everything.

Similarly, the course may seem to be stretching ahead for a year or more, no end in sight. Then, suddenly the end of the academic year is hurtling towards you. The whole course is over before you know it and you wonder where all that time went.

It feels like I only arrived here yesterday!!!

Mindful scheduling

Mindfulness is compatible with managing your time well and preparing ahead. When studying, that means being aware of everything you need to do and the time it will take. You can schedule study tasks cleverly across the year so that you are not caught out when time seems to speed up. Spreading tasks out more evenly means you won't be bored one minute and pressurized the next.

Be aware of assignment deadlines

As assignment deadlines are often set a long time in advance, don't get tricked into thinking you don't need to start work on them until later. It may be expected that you will work on several assignments at the same time, especially as deadlines approach – so it helps to complete some of the reading in advance, and to clear enough time in your diary. Take a look at your total assignment load early on and gain a sense of how much work might be involved. Draw up a schedule so that you know how you are going to juggle the work for each. This will avoid panic, stress and missed deadlines later in the year.

Time is like gold to students

It isn't just how you schedule time across the year that is important. It is also a question of:

- ~ How much time you put into your studies altogether
- ~ How much of that time is used really effectively.

Lack of time is one of the greatest barriers to student success, just as lack of money is a barrier to investing in a business. Whilst such investment doesn't always mean success, it is necessary. Studying additional hours doesn't always help (though it can) but you do need to put in at least the recommended hours and possibly more.

The required hours might already put pressure on your time, especially if you have other commitments, so it helps if you use all your study time effectively through remaining focused on what you need to do. Mindfulness practice strengthens your attentional abilities (see Chapters 37–9), which is an advantage when it comes to using precious study time well. Making good use of study time means it is easier to fit in all the reading, researching, thinking, creating, problem-solving, discussing, writing, checking, re-drafting and revising that you have to do.

Mindfulness or procrastination? Maybe later ...

At some point, most students grapple with procrastination – or putting things off until later. It is tempting, because of the amount of unscheduled study time. There always seems to be an inviting slice of 'later' available for doing things, until time runs out altogether.

Being successful at anything involves bringing our attention to what needs to be done, when it needs to be done – rather than rationalizing with ourselves that it will all be fine if we do it some other time. Mindfulness is useful because it trains the attention on 'now' rather than on the potential future with which procrastination entices us. We become aware, more quickly, of how our thoughts are finding ways of 'putting off' study tasks. We can then bring our awareness to this, and decide whether we would be better to just do it now. You can use mindfulness to transform procrastinating thoughts into immediate action.

👁 Observation: Awareness of study time

Over the next few days or weeks, bring your awareness to 'Time'. Does it seem to drag slowly or to race by? What makes it feel that way?

What proportion of your week is spent in active, focused study? How does that compare with course expectations of the time to spend on study?

Observe what proportion of your study time you waste. On what kinds of things do you waste that time? What triggers your time wasting? What kinds of study tasks do you tend to try and put off?

🧍 Reflection: Mindful use of study time

Consider your observations of your study time, above.

- ～ What do you do well already in managing study time effectively? How might you extend these good habits to other areas of study?
- ～ Why do you think you waste time and procrastinate when you do? Consider the role that aversions and delusions play (pages 127–42).

Things you can do

Managing time mindfully

Consider ☑ which, if any, of the following would make a difference to your studies

☐ Be clearer about everything I need to do across the year.

☐ Schedule tasks better, so that I can fit in everything I have to do.

☐ Be better at using my diary/planner.

☐ Spread tasks out more evenly so that I am not bored one minute and rushed the next.

☐ When there seem to be few study demands, identify things to prepare ahead for later.

☐ Make sure I am studying for at least the minimum hours expected.

☐ Be more aware of *when* I waste time unnecessarily. (What is it about those times in particular that prompts me to waste time?)

☐ Be more aware of *what* I do when I am wasting time. (When would be a better time to do those things? Do I need to do them at all?)

☐ Be more aware of the kinds of study tasks that prompt me to waste time or procrastinate, so that I can approach these differently.

☐ Enlist other people's support in helping me to use study time more effectively, such as by respecting my study time and not interrupting it.

☐ Set my study time up better, so that I am in a better state of mind for study (see Chapter 30).

☐ Find out more about time management (see Cottrell, *The Study Skills Handbook*).

Plan it out

1. Decide when and how you will put these into action.

2. If you have selected many options above, start with the most important three, then come back to others.

3. Schedule into your diary or planner when you will do these things and when you will check back to see that they have been done.

41

Reading mindfully

There can be an air of excitement about beginning a new subject, topic or assignment – it's a fresh start and everything seems possible. It can be energizing to search out and assemble the reading material, especially items recommended by the course. It isn't uncommon for students to be so enthusiastic that they purchase all the books on the reading list, or to become highly frustrated if all the books aren't immediately available through their college or university library. All too often, at some point between that initial enthusiasm and completing the course, reading can become a battleground.

It may seem too hard, too much, not what you expected.

You may get bored.

You forget what you read.

I know I wrote that quotation down somewhere...

You had found a quote or statistic that was exactly what you needed. You are sure you had written it down, but now you can't find it in your notes nor remember where you read it.

Other diversions can become more enticing so that you resent having to spend time reading instead.

Getting down to reading, selecting the right reading, getting through the reading, making sense of the reading, and drawing on reading appropriately – all are common difficulties when studying. This is where your mindfulness practice can make a difference, helping you to bring more awareness to your reading and in making effective use of your attentional resources.

'Mindless reading' — or reading 'on automatic'

It is not uncommon to find we have read paragraphs, or even several pages, without taking in a word of what we have read. Most students have long mastered the technical aspects of reading, such as recognizing words on a page, making reasonable guesses at unfamiliar words, pausing slightly at punctuation, even breathing in tune with the rhythm of what they read. You are probably so good at reading that you can do it 'on automatic' alongside other tasks such as listening to music, eating, walking, maybe even taking notes at the same time. You can combine the technical act of reading with comprehending the meaning of what you read and critiquing it.

The downside of such technical proficiency is that you can drift off into thoughts, or into focusing on a second task, without realizing. You cease to attend to the meaning of what you are reading. Your attention is not on abstracting what is relevant within the text.

This matters for students ...

For students, this can be especially frustrating as reading constitutes such a large part of study and available time. If your attention keeps drifting, this can have several unwanted consequences:

- It may not be obvious to you that you have missed out some essential information needed in order to understand and apply the material.
- It is likely that you will need to re-read passages or even pages.
- You lose precious time as a result – time that could have been spent on other things such as rest, socializing, family, work, sleep, exercise, sport, music, games.
- You waste time available for other aspects of study or that assignment.
- It can feel boring or frustrating going back over tasks for a second time, increasing the potential for impatience to finish and superficial reading rather than being fully focused and interested.

Reading more mindfully

Reading is an activity that can benefit from mindfulness in many ways:

1. From the accrued benefits of mindfulness practice
2. From a pre-reading 'awareness warm-up'
3. From increased self-awareness of responses to reading
4. From bringing awareness to mind-wandering
5. From reading mindfully as in 'everyday' mindfulness activities
6. From bringing Metta to your reading schedule.

1. Accrued benefits of mindfulness practice

Reading is a task that calls on cognitive skills that research shows benefit from meditation, such as focus, concentration, information processing and recall (see Chapter 37). If you build your practice over several weeks and continue it across your course, your reading persistence, as well as your understanding and recall of what you read, are likely to improve.

2. Pre-reading 'awareness warm-up'

- First do a brief study 'warm-up' as outlined in Chapter 30. Focus your attention on that, rather than thinking ahead about the reading yet.

- Open your eyes and come back to the room. Stretch a little.

- Bring your focus to the reading task ahead. Spend two or three minutes considering the task. Jot down the length of time you intend to read, and the kinds of information you intend to gain from your reading. As far as possible, phrase this as questions to which you will be searching out the answers. Decide how much detail you need to note down before the reading session is over, when you will write your notes, and the kinds of notes you will take.

- Note the time. Set a timer for the end of the reading session.

Use the evaluation below to give some initial consideration to your responses to reading.

Self-awareness for responses to reading

Consider these typical student responses to reading for their course. Identify ☑ any which are similar to your own – some or all of the time.

Responding with aversion to reading tasks

☐ **Refusal:** I don't like this topic/book/font/cover/writer/theory/lighting/room/seating etc. so I am not going to read this.

☐ **Excuses:** I don't want to re-read this. I don't really need to because …

☐ **Delays:** I should read this in the vacation but I'll wait until term begins.

☐ **Doing minimum:** I don't like this much so I'll read as little as possible.

☐ **Rushing it:** I'll read this quickly so I can get it out of the way.

☐ **Filtering it out:** I don't want to read this so I'll do it with the TV/radio/music in the background/while watching out for alerts on my phone, etc.

Responding with cravings

☐ **Grade-craving:** I must read everything or I won't get great grades.

☐ **Craving to outdo others:** I must be first to get all the library books.

☐ **Distraction-craving:** I really need to eat/drink/rest/etc. Right now! (even though I have barely started reading).

☐ **Craving alternatives:** I want to do something/anything else.

Delusion-like responses to reading tasks

☐ **Blaming the text:** It is obviously too boring/too long etc.

☐ **Misleading yourself:** It's OK to read less than I really need to.

☐ **Intellectual arrogance:** I'm so smart, I don't need to read this; I can wing it and nobody will notice I haven't read it.

☐ **Misguided emphasis:** I must read and note everything – just in case!

☐ **Pretending to read:** I am going through the motions of reading so I will probably remember it (despite taking nothing in).

Mindfulness when reading

3. Increased self-awareness of responses to reading

From time to time, bring your awareness to your 'inner script' for reading tasks, just as you did for observing negative inner chatter (Chapter 20).

Use the list above (page 164) to help you identify some of your more typical responses and jot down others that you notice in yourself. Observe how you phrase these responses – the details of your response are likely to vary a little from those above. Give a name or description to your responses, to help you pinpoint what is really going on for you.

Consider whether your response is the most skilful for you in your context. If not, write a different 'script' to inspire and guide your reading. Repeat this a few times, to anchor it in your mind. Write it down so you don't forget it. Put it in front of you on the desk.

Decide how to change your approach to reading so that you enjoy it more (see Chapter 32): your inner script may alter naturally in response.

 Reflection: Self-awareness of reading responses

- ～ What thoughts and behaviours do you bring to reading that undermine your focus and effectiveness for the task?
- ～ How well do you prepare, or 'set up', reading tasks before launching into them? What could you change about your preparation?

4. Bring awareness to mind-wandering

If you notice that your mind is drifting off when reading, acknowledge this, as you do when your mind drifts during meditation:

I am making judgements about whether the reading is difficult/boring.

I am thinking about dinner.   *I am thinking random thoughts.*

Sit with that awareness for a moment and take it in. Re-focus your attention. Find a specific question to focus on when you're reading, if needed.

5. Bring 'everyday mindfulness' to reading

Select your reading thoughtfully. Before starting to read, bring your awareness to the purpose of your reading. What do you need to find out? Jot down your questions where you can see them, to steer your reading.

Check the best place to locate that information: browse the text and its index to help locate what you need.

When reading, just read. Be fully present in the act of reading. Focus your awareness on understanding the text: What is the writer saying? What does that mean (in your words)? What is significant about that?

If you intend to make notes, read a relevant passage or section first. Pause. Consider how this is relevant to your reading purpose. Summarize this in your own words, aloud if possible. Note that down. Then find the next relevant section and repeat.

Use a 'Deliberately Mindful Moment' of 1–2 minutes, occasionally, to tune in to what you are doing. Notice whether you are:

- taking in what you are reading, understanding it and looking out for what is really significant
- reading purposefully – or drifting into general, unfocused reading
- making notes selectively – or noting everything or noting randomly
- keeping to schedule, or spending longer than planned – you may need a break
- wasting time: you may need to re-think your focus.

6. Bring Metta to your reading schedule

Check whether your reading schedule is too harsh, with too much reading forced into too short a time for you to remain focused.

- Spread reading tasks out across the week, term and year.
- Break reading into sections with scheduled breaks.
- If you read slowly, be more selective in which sections you read.
- Give yourself sufficient time to read and absorb complex and difficult material.

42

Word power:
Mindfulness of language

Building a good vocabulary

A good vocabulary is a bonus for most academic courses. Expanding your vocabulary, especially for language used in your subject discipline, assists understanding. A good vocabulary helps you to recognize the meaning of a sentence more quickly and to absorb new concepts and ideas at speed. With it, you can shape your thoughts more precisely, and communicate ideas more clearly. Conversely, poor expression and incorrect use of language hinder you in getting your message across. As a student, imprecise use of language and weak expression mean lower grades: your knowledge and ideas might be great but you must be able to express these well.

Just the right words ...

Using the correct word, even if an obscure one, brings greater precision, helping your reader or listener to understand exactly what you mean. Aim to write clearly, concisely and without jargon to get your message across. There is no need to use 100 words when 10 will do, nor to throw in unusual words just to sound clever. In academic life, specialist and sometimes obscure vocabulary is used with a purpose: to convey particular ideas in a precise way. Each word is used or, at least, should be used, because it has a specific meaning and using another word would change the intended meaning.

> ### 🔔 Reflection: Appreciating language ...
>
> ~ Do you take much notice of how other people express themselves?
> ~ Do you pay sufficient attention to how clearly and precisely you express what you have to say, both when speaking and writing?
> ~ When did you last test out whether your use of grammar, punctuation and vocabulary is as good as you imagine?
> ~ How do you go about building your word power currently?

Awareness of your response to language

We have observed already the power of core responses of craving, aversion and delusion. Not surprisingly, these also influence and reflect the way we use and respond to language. For example:

Cravings *I love using jargon and long words – it makes me feel better about what I have to say; I want to write more than the word limit – I have so much to say! I want to sound clever so I will use lots of jargon and complex sentences to give that impression.*

Aversions *I hate 'big words' – so I won't expand my vocabulary. I hate people who use big words! I don't like to use my own words in assignments because I don't think I express myself very well.*

Delusion *It's boring to check your work for grammar and punctuation – so I won't bother much about that. It doesn't really matter how I express it – they'll know what I mean!*

 **Observation: Encountering new vocabulary**

Take note of how you respond to words you come across that you don't understand, whether spoken or in texts. For example, do you:

- Take pleasure in coming across a new word?
- Note down the word so you can look it up and learn it?
- Repeat it in your mind, to add it to your own vocabulary?

Notice whether your responses indicate that you are open and interested in language and keen to know how you can use it more effectively. Are your responses really helpful to you?

Reflection: Developing awareness of language

- ～ What could you do now to build your word power?
- ～ Are there any other changes you could make in your attitude towards language that would benefit your studies?
- ～ Do your tutors make any comments in their feedback on your work that suggest areas for strengthening your use of language?

43

Mindfulness when writing assignments

Writing isn't a natural process: it was invented. It doesn't always come naturally to students to produce a good piece of writing. Whilst it can be very satisfying to complete an assignment, it is common for students to resist the writing process: it isn't unusual to put off writing an assignment for as long as possible, even when the reading, research and thinking are done. Our minds can be great at providing us with reasons and excuses for not starting to write, for not sticking with it once begun, and for not creating the right conditions to produce a good piece of work.

Mindfulness practice helps us to be more aware of thought processes that are impeding our writing and to take charge of unskilful thoughts. We can become better at catching unhelpful thoughts before they become a feeling, attitude or habit to which we then attach.

👤 Skilful thought, skilful writing

Below are some typical ways that we allow our thoughts to divert ourselves from writing and from being fully present in the act of writing.

- ~ Identify ☑ whether these, or similar kinds of thoughts, are true of you
- ~ Consider how skilful you are at catching and managing such thoughts at an early stage.

☐ 'It should be easy …'

Writing is an art. Like any art, it takes thought, time, work and will-power. It may flow easily, but more often it takes a lot of re-working to get it just right. The road to the final draft can be, at times, fun, fascinating, informative and empowering but it can also be frustrating. That is true whether you are an established author or a student working on an assignment. So:

- ~ There will be intellectual challenge – accept that as a given
- ~ Don't assume it is easier for everyone else

- There may be times when your thoughts are tangled and the writing sounds awful when you read it back. This is just part of the process.

☐ 'I am a bad writer …'

Such phrases aren't helpful when writing as they direct the mind to consider that the task cannot be done. There are more useful ways of directing your mind when there is writing to be done. So:

- Take the 'I' out of the equation for a while.
- Bring your focus to your breath, as you would in meditation. A quiet meditation can help calm and prepare your mind for writing.
- Then let the writing itself be your focus. Consider what is needed so that the piece of writing is clear, informative, fit for purpose, complete.
- This generates tasks – things you can do. Bring your attention to those tasks rather than to yourself as the person doing the writing.

☐ 'I don't know where to start'

Every piece of writing starts from a different place: there isn't a given starting line. There are many thousands of options, so you get to decide. One thing to keep in mind is that 'starting to write' an assignment isn't the same as producing 'the start' of your assignment. So:

- Be prepared for the first thing that you write to end up in the middle or end of the assignment if it fits there better.
- Find a 'stimulus' to get you writing. Read your notes or the relevant parts of one or more texts to help generate ideas.
- Choose just one point as an initial focus: concentrate on that first.
- Frame the idea in your head about what you want to write: what is the point you want to make? Write it down.
- Then find the stimulus for your next point.

☐ 'I get distracted easily'

Again, this is a common problem. Use the tools at your disposal. So:

- Take a few minutes for a 'warm-up' (page 111) before settling down to study. This can help concentration during the study session ahead.

- If you can't get going, or come to a halt, take a few minutes to step back and clarify what you want to get done in the time available to you today, or even for the next half hour. Consider how to get to that point.
- Pause to re-focus when you feel your mind is drifting or goes blank. Use awareness of the breath to restore calm alertness.
- Become aware of any recurring distractions and take steps to remove or manage these so they don't get in the way of your writing.

☐ 'It would be much easier if …'

It is easy to come up with external factors to blame for why we aren't writing. We can spend a lot of time distracting ourselves from actually writing by finding reasons for why it is difficult. Even if the excuses are reasonable and true, ultimately, it doesn't get words on the page. We can either take steps to address those external factors so they don't hinder our writing or, if that really isn't possible, work with what we have got. At some point, we have to get on and write anyway; it will be up to us how soon we do this and how much time we waste wishing things were different. So:

- If you have really identified a way of making writing easier for you, follow through and put that idea in place. Otherwise, recognize the thought as an unhelpful distraction at this point.
- Bring your thoughts back to the present task. Let yourself be fully present in your writing for now.

☐ 'I can't hear myself think …'

Sometimes, there are so many competing ideas, facts, opinions, self-doubts, potential phrases that you might write or have just written, all buzzing in your head that you can't think clearly. That can make it feel difficult to write well. So:

- Use awareness of the breath for a few minutes to still your mind. It is likely that all that 'noise' will try to intrude. Don't worry about that. Just notice yourself noticing the stream of thoughts – that will put a little distance between them and you so that you are less entangled in them.
- Acknowledge thoughts as they arise, just as in meditation. Then let them drift away to sit on a shelf until you are ready for them.

- Sit for a few moments longer in stillness, not thinking about work. Give your brain a chance to let the important ideas come to the surface.

- In your calmer state, decide on a focus for the next half hour. You can return to other competing priorities later.

☐ 'I can't express my ideas in writing'

It can be difficult to combine, all-at-once, the various thought processes and actions that translate your knowledge into writing. It is a complex task to select all the most pertinent points, structure them into the right sequence, and link them together to produce a piece of writing that has a point, is clear and fit for purpose. It is unlikely you can do that well in your first draft. So:

- Recognize that there are different stages. Take them one-by-one if you need to, bringing full awareness to each. This can clear your thinking and help concentration.

- Get your initial thought down, however clumsily written. You then have something to work with.

- Break complex ideas into component parts, and write a short phrase or sentence about each. This will help each point to stand out clearly.

- If you have too many short sentences, read these through and decide which are the most logical to combine into fewer longer sentences.

- Keep checking for clarity. If anything sounds confusing or contorted, divide it into clear segments. It may be less elegant, but the priority is to make your points clearly so that your reader can understand what you are trying to say.

- For student assignments, unless these are meant to be creative, expressive or reflective, cut out anything that is rambling, anecdotal, or tangential to your central argument and key points.

☐ 'I don't want to cut these words' (even if they are not really relevant)

When we are writing, our imaginations can get caught up with interesting facts, ideas and opinions. These may be easier to write about. You may find they account for almost everything you first write down for your assignment. As a result, much of what you have written might not be relevant. That is fine – as long as you are strict at editing. For student assignments, you usually have to write to the point, in a given number of words, to address a specific question or issue. You only gain marks for relevant points. Spending too many words on one aspect probably means you are losing marks somewhere else. So:

- Be ruthless in analysing what you have written to see whether it is relevant. If not, cut it out.

- Is it just an 'interesting aside'? If so, it is probably wasting valuable words from your permitted total. Edit it out.

- If you are hesitating, ask yourself what points are really central to this assignment? What will tutors be expecting? What do you think are the key points to get across? Then ask yourself how what you have written illustrates or explains those central points. If it doesn't, cut!

- Even if the material is relevant, check whether you have used a disproportionate amount of the permitted word limit on some aspects. If so, re-write in a more succinct style, editing out excess material.

☐ 'I just can't do it!'

When writing to a deadline, such as for student assignments, if the ideas don't come together easily in writing, this can lead to self-doubt or panic. This in turn can create a vicious cycle: it is harder to write when your brain and body are panicking. At such times, you draw on a part of the brain that is prioritizing your safety rather than intellectual reasoning or creativity. So:

- Even if time is pressured, take a few moments to bring yourself out of panic mode. Bring your attention back to your breath.

- If you have time, add 'Just now': 'I can't do this, just now.' Take a break.

- There will be parts of the task you can do. Identify what these are. Tell yourself that you can do these – you can. Do those first, as this will make you feel more confident. There are fewer things to worry about once some tasks are done.

- Identify the next least difficult task and do as much of that as you can. It is likely that if you work through tasks steadily, in small steps, you will get to the end. If you get to a point where you are really stuck, talk to your tutor or a support worker.

☐ 'I wrote it, so it feels part of me now ...'

After labouring to complete a piece of writing, it is easy to become over-attached to what you have produced. The last thing you may feel like doing is putting a line through writing that took a lot of effort. You may need to say goodbye to your fine words. Leave your writing for a day or so and re-read it: you may then feel differently about it. If you want a good piece of writing, you must be willing to 'cut' and edit. So:

- Don't get too attached to what you have written.
- Be prepared to re-write a phrase, a sentence, a page, to start the whole piece again if needed – and then to do so again, and maybe again.
- Schedule enough time for multiple re-writes.
- Start your assignments as early as possible, so you have enough time available to re-draft and fine-tune your writing.

☐ 'I can't submit this – it isn't perfect yet'

Your 'inner critic' can be an invaluable friend for pointing out where your work can be improved. That is great for helping you address weak spots so that you have a better piece of work in which you can take pride and which helps your audience to access your message. If the inner critic is too strong, though, you will never complete a piece of writing. For students, the consequences would be severe: it would mean lower grades or not completing your course, as well as the sense of dissatisfaction.

A balanced perspective is important. Assignments are rarely perfect. Most authors can see things to improve in their work, even when they have crafted it for a long time or it is in print: it could always be cleverer, wittier, more precise, more informative. It can help to bear that in mind when grappling with your own piece. So:

- Do continue to develop your writing process so that you are better at recognizing when your work could be written more elegantly, with greater clarity and precision, or in a more informative way.
- Improve your awareness of the point at which your work is 'good enough' for your purpose – given the time available.
- If it is an assignment and the deadline has arrived, submit what you have written rather than handing it in late.

Find the pleasure in writing

Enjoy the process

It is easier to enjoy writing if you are fully present in the process, bringing awareness to the stages involved, your ideas that are forming, the phrases you are generating, the steps you can take to improve it further.

Leave sufficient time to enjoy the process

The creative process can be very enjoyable – especially if you don't have to rush it. It can also be calming to go through your writing thoughtfully, considering ways to improve a phrase here and there, spotting errors and correcting them, finding more succinct ways to say something so that you release words to use to make a new point. Through such re-writing, you can see your work improve before your eyes, through your own actions.

Write just for pleasure occasionally

If you are always writing for others, or for marked assignments, that can drain enjoyment from the act of writing. If you find that is the case, write a little every day just for yourself. Write a blog; keep a diary or journal; write poems, raps, short stories, whatever sparks your interest.

Take pleasure in your previous pieces of writing

When you are writing for an assignment, it is sensible to read your work in terms of how it will be read by your tutor and how it might be graded. However, this can detract from the pleasure of just writing. Come back to your assignments at a later date, and re-read them without worrying about the grade. Bring your awareness to the words on the page as expressions of your own ideas. Find the sections or phrases you like the best and let yourself enjoy these: you may feel happier about future writing tasks.

Celebrate progress

The more you work at your writing, the better you become. It is easy to lose track of how far you have progressed. Do look back over your writing. Notice the ways in which your writing has changed and improved.

Writing mindfully: Things you can do

Set yourself up well for your writing sessions through a short mindfulness meditation or exercise – even if just for a few moments.

Let yourself be fully present in the task of writing, bringing your attention back to the process, and not worrying about what you haven't done yet.

Be mindful of the ego: focus on the process rather than on your identity as a 'good' or 'bad' writer. Recognize that writing is a challenging activity and don't dramatize the difficulties as personal just to you.

Bear in mind that all writing starts with just getting something on the page. From there, you can add, adapt, edit, fine-tune.

Writing doesn't usually come from nowhere: it requires inspiration, such as stimulus gained from reading, observation, research, personal interest and exposure to a variety of ideas. Give your mind suitable chunks of relevant stimulus material to work with.

Become aware of unskilful thought patterns that may arise, such as rationalizations and excuses for not writing. Recognize them for what they are. Use a few moments of mindful breathing to let these evaporate. Bring your attention back just to writing.

Refine your awareness of how your mind lets you become distracted, and the kinds of distractions it chooses. Take steps to remove or manage those distractions so that they don't interfere with your writing.

Use your inner critic to improve your writing, but be aware of where it tries to overstep the mark, so that it doesn't disempower you as a writer.

When your mind is racing or cluttered, bring your awareness back to the breath for a while to let the buzzing subside and clarity emerge.

Don't let fear of failure nor over-perfectionism get in the way of writing or submitting your work. Be mindful of your purpose in writing; direct your time, thoughts and writing accordingly. If you have an audience, write in the appropriate style for them. If you have a word limit, stick to it. If you have a time limit, plan towards it, submitting your work when time is up.

You are the author of your own work: search out the pleasure in that.

44

Using tutor feedback mindfully

Although students generally say they value feedback on their work, every year, many thousands of pieces of marked student work are left uncollected. Many students find out their grades from noticeboards or online, but don't look at their work again. All the advice, suggestions, corrected assumptions and errors, the hints, guidance on ways to improve, all the praise and smiley faces go unheeded, ending up in a shredder. In other cases, students do collect their work but don't make systematic use of the advice. They either don't want feedback or persuade themselves they don't need it.

🧘 Reflection: My attitude towards tutor feedback

Read the comments below. Which, if any, reflect thoughts you have had about tutor feedback? How much use do you make of tutor feedback currently?

Aversion to tutor feedback	Delusions about feedback
I don't agree with the comments on my work.	*My work is already as good as it is going to be.*
I don't want feedback.	*The tutors always write a lot on my work – they just don't like me.*
I feel defeated by tutor criticism.	*I don't really need feedback.*
I don't like feedback that tells me what is missing in my assignments or where I went wrong.	*It is a waste of time reading the feedback as the next assignment will be different.*
My tutors' comments depress me – I'm just going to ignore them.	*I have read through the feedback so I will remember it next time.*
	I have read the feedback. I don't need to think about how I use it.

What if ...

What if your tutor's feedback could make a difference to a future assignment, or to your understanding of the issues you studied?

What if you are incredibly lucky to get such expert insights?

What if the feedback is designed to help you succeed?

What if you welcomed feedback and criticism, as a great way of finding out how to improve your performance for the rest of your life?

What if you used the feedback to improve all your future work?

Things you can do

Always read through your work once it has been marked.

Read feedback with focused attention. Make sure you understand the point your tutor is making. Ask for clarification if it doesn't make sense.

Use the feedback to become more aware of what you do well already and of how you can improve.

Assume that feedback contains value for you and that there are things you could learn: search out clues about how to do things better.

Use pages in your student diary to maintain a record of comments you receive. Look for trends in the feedback.

Make a habit of reading back over your record of tutor comments before you start each assignment, and again before you submit it.

Be systematic in the way you make use of feedback. Identify what you need to do to improve, then follow through on that.

Plan it out

1. Schedule into your diary or planner when to collect your marked work and when you will go through it systematically.
2. Write yourself reminders for making use of the advice contained with tutor feedback for your future assignments.

45

Mindfulness for tests, exams and assessment

To achieve a university or college qualification, you will probably encounter tests, exams and other forms of formal assessments, such as essays, reports and dissertations. It is natural to want to do well when you have put time, energy and money into your course; that can also bring pressure. For many students, exams and marked assessments are high on both their aversion and grasping scales: they don't like them but want high grades from them.

Many students delude themselves about how bad or good they are at assessments. Some are convinced that they will fail, even though most students who stick with a course do then pass it. Others persuade themselves that they will do well despite minimal effort, and are then shocked when they do not achieve as well as they wanted.

It *is* possible to love exams and assessments: there are people who prefer these to other parts of their course. They enjoy the increased sense of purpose, the intense learning, and mastering their subject. They like the challenge, the interest in grappling with difficult questions, and the awareness that they are producing good answers. You *can* approach exams and assessment with feelings other than dread.

My attitude towards assessment

Use this self-evaluation to consider your approach to exams and marked assignments. Select ☑ any of the following statements that apply to you.

☐ 1. I hate doing assignments that are going to be graded

☐ 2. I hate exams

☐ 3. I'll never get good grades

☐ 4. I'm no good at exams

☐ 5. I'm no good at coursework

☐ 6. I avoid exams when I can

☐ 7. I feel miserable when revising

☐ 8. I wind myself up about exams

☐ 9. I get nervous about submitting my assignments

☐ 10. I get very anxious about exams

☐ 11. I would rather avoid exams but I take them in my stride

☐ 12. I want to do well but it isn't the end of the world if I don't

☐ 13. I learn more when I have exams

☐ 14. I am realistically optimistic about my grades

☐ 15. I exercise to work off excess adrenalin when revising

☐ 16. I devise a good strategy so I feel more in control

☐ 17. I prepare well for exams so I will always know I did my best

☐ 18. I enjoy preparing for exams

☐ 19. I like the challenge of doing well at exams

Reflection: My attitude towards assessment

~ How helpful to you is your attitude towards assessment?

~ If you selected mainly statements above in the low numbers, how could you shift your attitude so that it better reflects the attitudes associated with statements in the higher numbers? What would you need to do differently? Who or what could help?

How to feel better about exams and assessment

1. Understand their purpose

Exams and assignments are just routine parts of a course, not monsters out to get you. They provide a good focus for learning course material more intensely, motivating you to devise mnemonics when you might not otherwise bother. You don't need to do brilliantly just to pass, and passing already takes you a long way. Getting a good grade is then a bonus.

2. Recognize that they are not a mystery

Contrary to some myths, exams are not designed to trick you. Tutors want their students to succeed. They provide lots of clues about what you need to demonstrate through assessment – even through the way they design and deliver the course. You can pass exams, and do well, with a good exam strategy.

3. Adopt the right attitude

Your attitude is something that you can control. You will feel better or worse about exams depending on which approach you take. You don't need to love exams, but you don't need to hate or fear them either.

4. Prepare well in advance

You will feel better about exams if you know you have covered the course material and tested yourself on it before the exam. Go through past papers carefully. Test yourself under exam conditions, like a 'dress rehearsal'. Good technique and strategy make a difference: if you need to improve these, use a dedicated exam skills book, such as Cottrell (2012).

Mindfulness for exams and assessment

Use techniques, abilities and qualities you are developing through your mindfulness practice to help you through assessments and exam periods.

Approach exams and assignments with equanimity

~ Aim to maintain a calm approach to exams and assessments – take them in your stride, rather than getting too excited or nervous.

~ Use the 'warm up to study' exercise on page 111 before settling into sessions to prepare for assessment and exams. Draw on other techniques such as mindful walking (page 89) if you prefer.

~ If you find yourself getting agitated or distressed whilst working on assessments or revising for exams, recognize the thoughts and emotions as you would in mindfulness meditation (see Chapter 18). Bring awareness to your breathing to re-establish calm before continuing with your study.

Bring awareness to your 'inner chatter'

Be aware of your inner chatter with respect to forthcoming assessments or exams (see Chapter 20). Attend to what it suggests about your approach and potential weaknesses. Are you overly optimistic, such that this reduces your motivation to get on with revising, preparing, practising and learning new skills? If so, check that you have a good exam or assignment strategy. Stick to this so that you have good grounds for your optimism.

Alternatively, notice whether your inner chatter is generating anxiety or a sense of dread. If so, bring your awareness to those feelings and let them subside. Be aware that though your feelings are real, what you dread doesn't need to be. For now, it is just a thought. You can change thoughts so that they work better for you.

Touch back in to the enjoyment

There is no reason why exams and assessments have to be about doom and gloom. For assignments, foster interest and enjoyment as you would for other aspects of your studies (see Chapter 32). Look for ways of bringing interest and fun to exam preparation. Read something that brings a new angle to the topic. Use colourful images and devise mnemonics that make you smile as well as remember the material. Set yourself quizzes to check your recall and to gain a greater sense of being in control of exam outcomes. Set up study sessions with others, perhaps after a meal together: exam preparation can be a social activity.

Bring focus to your exam preparation

Mindfulness helps to train the attention (see Chapters 37–8) so just maintaining your practice should help both in staying focused when revising or studying and in noticing when your attention has drifted. You can bring your awareness to the breath at any stage: even a short spell of 15–20 seconds can help re-establish your focus during revision sessions.

Bring Metta to your preparation

Take special care of yourself during pressurized exam and assessment periods, respecting your need for sleep, nutrition and relaxed downtime. Be aware of whether you are working too hard, staying up too late, missing sleep or studying when you are too exhausted to learn anything.

Notice if you start getting caught up in negative feelings about things you 'should have done' rather than focusing on revision or assessment tasks you can get on with now. Self-blame and nursing negative feelings may not feel great but they can still be ways of putting off work for a while.

- Bring some compassion to the side of you that you feel 'messed up' or could have done things differently. Let your negative self-criticism drift away.

- Self-blaming won't get the job done so focus instead on a plan to get through the task in a manageable and realistic way, asking for help if you need it.

- It may help you to write down your negative feelings about yourself. That can get them out of your system, leaving you to focus on your work in a more neutral state of mind.

Mindfulness on the day of an exam

Calmness for the exam

Before you leave home. Start the day well by using a short Mindfulness of Breathing or Metta meditation to steady the breathing and emotions, and start to focus your attention.

On your way to the exam. Use mindful walking or mindful travel meditations (pages 89 and 92). You may wish to revise during your journey or to check final details. If so, just find a minute here and there to bring awareness to your breathing.

At the start of the exam. Whilst people are settling down and papers are being distributed, use awareness of the breath to gain calm and focus.

During the exam. If you start to feel anxious, pause for a minute or two. Stabilize your breathing with a few deep breaths, as you would do before a meditation. Imagine that you are breathing in calm with each in-breath. Release tension, anxiety or fear on each out-breath, imagining these leaving through your feet, into the floor and flowing away.

Remain focused during the exam

If you notice your attention has drifted or your mind goes blank, bring your attention back to the exam paper, just as you would re-focus during meditation. Read the next question.

If you were mid-way through answering a question, re-read that question. Browse quickly through what you have written, and think about what you want to say next.

If you can't think of an answer straight away, jot down anything you recall on the topic: this may jog other information back into memory. If not, leave that question for now and come back to it later.

46

Mindful management of stress and set-backs

With all the demands and challenges of higher education, a large proportion of students experience unhelpfully high levels of stress and anxiety at some point (Deckro et al., 2002; NUS, 2015).

Whilst some stress is helpful in charging us up to face challenges and feel excitement at doing so, too much impairs our ability to concentrate, think clearly, and do well at our studies (Hill, 1984; Keogh et al., 2006). Feeling anxious or depressed makes it harder to filter out what is relevant or irrelevant. This adds to distractibility, making it difficult to focus, organize, stay on task, and remember things (Bremner and Narayan, 1998). All of this can have severe effects on our capacity to learn and to demonstrate our learning in high-pressure contexts such as exams and presentations.

Being able to manage stress to reasonable levels for most of the time is an advantage to study. Although mindfulness is not, specifically, a stress-management tool, many people find that it is effective in relieving excess stress and anxiety, and bringing calm.

What does research tell us about mindfulness and stress?

Daily practice reduces study-related stress

In studies, participants who received just eight weeks of daily mindfulness meditation reported less fatigue, negativity and inertia after completing stressful tasks (Levy et al., 2012). Training in relaxation techniques did not produce the same effects. The researchers felt that mindfulness resulted in a chain of effects that helped those who meditated to become more competent learners. As a result of feeling competent, they then experienced less stress.

Daily mindfulness meditation

▼

Less task-switching, greater concentration, greater ability to stay on task and better memory for the details of the task

▼

Greater sense of personal competence

▼

Reduced stress and negativity

Mindfulness helps students manage cortisol levels

At times of stress, we produce the hormone cortisol. Over time, cortisol can do damage to the body. In a study in which Chinese undergraduates were given a stressful lab test, students who meditated for 20 minutes a day over 5 days showed less anxiety and better mood than those who didn't. Their levels of cortisol were found to go down more quickly after the lab test was over (Tang et al., 2007).

Mindfulness reduces stressful rumination

A study involving students from medical, nursing, pre-medical and pre-health studies found that a month of mindfulness meditation not only improved mood and reduced distress but also increased students' ability to avoid becoming immersed in negative and distracting thoughts. Mindfulness helped students to cope with distress and better manage the stresses of higher education that otherwise maintain high levels of anxiety (Jain et al., 2007; Shapiro et al., 2007).

Using mindfulness to reduce stress

Use your awareness of the breath

When you notice that you are feeling stressed, bring your awareness to your breath, just as you do when meditating. Follow your breath for a few moments whilst you just observe how you are breathing.

You may notice that you are breathing is quick and shallow. If so, take a few deep breaths to stabilize your breathing, focusing especially on breathing out fully. That will help to prevent you from hyperventilating. You may find it helps to blow out sharply two or three times, and then let the breath fill your lungs slowly, before returning to just watching the breath.

Focusing on your breath can calm you and enable you to maintain a greater steadiness of response. It puts some distance between you and the cause of stress, allowing you to observe it more clearly.

When you feel calmer, bring your awareness to the situation that caused you anxiety. Focus on your own thoughts and actions in the situation, how you responded to what was happening, rather than thinking about what others said or did or what was wrong about the situation. Doing this does not mean that you are blaming yourself. It just allows you to reconsider how you could respond in ways that leave you feeling calmer.

Draw on your self-metta

When you are feeling stressed, whatever the cause, some part of you needs kindness and compassion. You don't have to indulge in macho behaviour, pretending you don't need anything. Nor do you need to indulge in self-pity. Instead, bring awareness to your feelings, whatever they might be, naming and acknowledging them.

During the day, if you aren't in a situation where you can do a sitting Metta meditation, take a few minutes when you can, such as in the library or walking between venues. Just notice your feelings and bring some kindness towards them.

As you do in meditation, repeat a phrase to help you to tune in to feelings of self-compassion. Either choose something suitable to the context or use a general phrase such as 'Let me be calm. Let me be happy.'

Managing stressful moments

The day can be filled with minor events that create irritation, petty resentments, or anxiety about potential outcomes: the queue in the cafeteria moves really slowly; your bus or train is late; a lecture is cancelled at the last minute; someone keeps interrupting when you are speaking; the book you want isn't available.

Such moments may not seem much in themselves but can add to general levels of stress as well as making pre-existing stress more difficult to manage. They may become unwanted outlets for releasing anger and impatience that has been building. At such times:

- Pause. Remind yourself: 'I have tools that I can use, in mindfulness and Metta, to help manage this situation.'

- It is easy to lose compassion for others in such moments. Although it may be hard, Metta can help at such times. Understanding other people's positions shifts your perspective a little, reducing the sting of the situation and providing a route to greater calm.

- Become aware of your stress triggers, using the observation below. Take time to reflect on your observations in order to understand those trigger points and manage your stress response better.

👁 Observation: Mindfulness of stress triggers

From time to time, bring your awareness to the range of incidents that got on your nerves during the day. Notice such things as:

- What occurred that triggered a sense of stress or anxiety?
- What kinds of things seemed to add most to your stress levels?
- How did you respond at such times: what did you think, do, say?
- How did you feel emotionally? (Irritable? Angry? Overwhelmed?)
- Where did you hold stress physically in your body?
- How did Mindfulness of Breathing or Metta help?

Jot down your observations. Come back to these and use the reflection below to help understand your triggers better.

Reflection: Understanding your stress triggers

Look over your observations to see what you can learn from them:

- What kinds of things seem to trigger feelings of stress for you?
- How do you tend to experience stress, physically and emotionally?
- Is your stress triggered more when you lack sleep, eat poorly, don't get much exercise, or when you are around certain people?
- What could you do to reduce the effect of these stress triggers, whilst still maintaining your studies?

Be aware of self-pressure

You may find that you are putting yourself under too much pressure when an assignment is due or just before an exam. It can be hard to juggle everything, especially when you have other commitments such as a job, family responsibilities, arts performances or sports fixtures coming up, or if you are filling your diary with many activities to build your CV.

If you don't get the grades you want for an assignment, miss an important deadline or mess up an exam question, it is easy to fall prey to negative self-criticism and self-doubt. If you experience this:

- Set priorities. Not everything has to be done at once. The consequences of re-scheduling some things, or not doing them at all, will be less for some things than others.
- Maintain perspective. If that feels difficult, talk to a student counsellor, tutor or someone else you trust.
- Tune back in to finding enjoyment – you experience stress less when you enjoy what you do and find satisfaction in it (Chapter 32).

Reflection: Self-pressure

- What kinds of pressures do you put yourself under?
- What practical steps can you take to reduce such pressures?

Other things you can do

Mindful use of social media

- Avoid content that you know makes you feel stressed.
- Don't engage in arguments and negative exchanges.
- Set specific times for checking social media; stick to these.
- Reduce the overall time you spend on social media, to ease pressure on your time for study and other commitments.

Spend time with others

- Don't spend all your time studying on your own.
- Find a study group, mentor or student peer-learning group.
- Find a friend to study alongside in the library or to meet up with during breaks in study.
- Maintain a good family or social life outside of study.
- Pursue at least one interest beyond study.
- Join a mindfulness group.

Focus on the physical

Bring your awareness to where you experience stress physically. Notice what it feels like and how that feeling changes or subsides. If you wish, direct the breath or feelings of kindness to that area.

Exercise has been shown to reduce anxiety, so use sport, dancing or even housework to use up excess adrenalin and for a change of scene and outlook.

Use available support

Don't be afraid to speak to student support staff if you feel over-stressed – a lot of students use these services. The staff will be familiar with the stresses that affect students and are used to maintaining confidentiality. They may offer counselling, support groups, guidance, or referral to other services if you wish.

Do you need more help?

If you are experiencing high levels of stress, anxiety or depression, and have found using mindfulness helpful, you might want to explore Mindfulness Based Stress Reduction therapies. Your college or university Counselling services or your General Practitioner (GP) should be able to advise.

See also

- 'Finding the joy in study' (Chapter 32)
- 'Taking care of your mind' (page 96)

Part

4

Records and reflections

47

Mindfulness and reflection

Reflection for academic courses

Increasingly, academic courses place value on critical reflection. This requires you to think about your experience in an intellectual way – to consider what has happened, to use research and theory to throw light on your experience. On creative courses, you may be asked to express your reflections on experience in an artistic way – to bring imagination to bear, to find new metaphors, new syntheses of ideas and styles. For care, business and other professional courses, you draw critically on your experience and apply it to workplace practice. Similarly, mindfulness practice can benefit from constructive self-reflection.

Mindfulness practice itself does not involve reflection

During mindfulness practice, the attention is focused on being in the moment, observing it rather than reflecting about it or extracting meaning. If you are feeling angry, you just register that this is the case, without looking to understand why. If you feel frustrated by your study or annoyed by a tutor, you register that, rather than trying to get to the bottom of why you feel like that, or who is right and who is wrong. This experiential processing has been described as 'decentring' as you observe experience rather than considering whether this is good or bad from your personal perspective (Brown et al., 2007; Teasdale, 1999).

The usefulness of decentred observation

This has benefits in everyday life as it helps you create a mental distance between observing an event and reacting to emotions that it might evoke. Over time, this practice can be useful for remaining emotionally disengaged in difficult work or life situations, rather than being drawn into arguments and disputes as a result of personal biases, assumptions, previous personal experiences or personal anxieties and concerns. It helps to maintain a clear head for observing what is actually happening minute by minute and bring clearer awareness of mind to dealing with the issues.

Reflecting on mindfulness practice

Although you don't set out to undertake reflection during mindfulness practice, it is a good idea to reflect at a later point.

Take a few moments to reflect after each meditation or exercise.

- Jot down in a journal or notebook anything you find interesting or useful, as and when this feels worth doing.
- You may find it useful to draw on the prompts on page 197.

Put some time aside every now and again to consider how your practice is going, whether you want to change anything about it, and whether it is having any effect on you. Be mindful that, if you leave this too long, you might not remember much that is useful. If you wish, use the prompts for reflecting on your meditation practice (page 198).

Recording time spent in mindfulness

You don't have to keep a record of time spent in mindful activity, but you may find it useful. If so, there are record sheets you can use on pages 200–3.

What counts as mindful activity, for recording purposes?

Here, mindful activity is taken to mean:

- Mindfulness of Breathing or Metta meditation (see Chapters 18 and 21)
- Mindfulness exercises (Chapters 13–17)
- Activity where you bring a consciously mindful approach to everyday activities or study (Chapter 26)
- Deliberately Mindful Moments (DMMs – see page 95)
- Two-minute meditations (page 94)

⬉ Prompts and Templates

The resources on the pages that follow can be downloaded for personal use from the companion site to the book at www.macmillanihe.com/mindfulness.

(a) 'To Do' Checklist

How to use the book on page xx refers to this checklist to help you keep track of what you have done so far, should you wish to do so.

	To do...	Done or underway
1	Read Part 1. Become aware of what mindfulness is about, where it started, and what you can expect.	
2	If relevant for you, take note of page 40 and put the right support in place.	
3	Read Preparation (page 46) to get ready.	
4	Do the Starter exercises (pages 47–60) to gain a sense of what to expect.	
4a	Starter exercise: Just noticing (pages 49–50)	
4b	Starter exercise: Seeing with new eyes (pages 51–2)	
4c	Starter exercise: Appreciating stillness (pages 53–6)	
4d	Starter exercise: Awareness of body and breath (pages 57–60)	
5	Learn and practise 'Mindfulness of Breathing' (page 62).	
6	Introduce the four stages into 'Mindfulness of Breathing' (pages 63–4).	
7	Learn and practise Metta (Chapters 21–22).	
8	Consider finding others with whom to practise and share your experience (Chapter 24).	
9	Establish your practice (Chapter 23).	

	To do...	Done or underway
10	Look ahead to Part 3. Read and consider how Chapters 29–46 apply to your studies.	
11	Start to apply mindfulness to your studies, drawing on relevant chapters in Part 3.	
12	Look at ways of building a mindful attitude through incorporating it into some everyday activities.	
13	Have a go at mindfulness of walking.	
14	Have a go at mindfulness when eating.	
15	Have a go at mindfulness when standing in line.	
16	Have a go at mindfulness for journeys.	
17	Have a go at using the Two-minute meditations (page 94).	
18	Have a go at Deliberately Mindful Moments (DMMs, page 95).	
19	Look for opportunities to use mindfulness in your everyday life and study. You can do so at any time.	
20	Record and reflect on your experience when this seems useful. Jot down observations or insights. Decide what is working well for you.	
21	Read back over Part 1, especially pages 33–6. Reflect on what these mean for you now.	
22	Keep practising. Restart your daily practice if you drift from it.	

(b) Reflecting on meditation sessions

Read through the following prompts. Reflect on those that are most relevant to your current practice. If you think it useful, jot down your thoughts.

How do you feel about the meditation?	Interested? Keen to keep going? Enjoying it? Enthusiastic? Irritated? Impatient to achieve obvious changes more quickly? Reluctant? Resistant? Something else? Don't know?
Are you judging your responses to the meditation?	Are you pleased with yourself for how well it is going? Criticizing yourself? Defensive about your attitude? Or not aware of any inner voice of judgement at all?
What about other feelings?	What do you feel at this moment? Happy? Content? Sad? Angry? Anxious? Joyful? Serene? Worried? Don't know?
What do you notice about your body when meditating?	Do you feel comfortable? Relaxed or tense? Upright, leaning or slumped? Neck and shoulders feel supported or heavy? Limbs comfortable or stiff? Not sure?
What about your surroundings for meditation?	Hot, warm, cool or cold? Is there any breeze? Noisy or quiet? Are there people around? Is it wet or dry outside? Is the furniture comfortable?
What do you notice about your breathing?	Is it quiet or noisy? Is it deep or shallow? Fast or slow? Easy or laboured? A pleasure? Or uncomfortable? Through the nose or mouth or both? Are you able to just observe it? Do you try to change or control it?
Are you focused?	Are you able to remain focused on the object of the meditation (breathing, walking, etc.)? What thoughts arise? Are you able to let go of these? Which thoughts distract you and draw you in so you forget the meditation?

(c) Themes for reflecting on meditation practice

Read through the following prompts. Reflect on those that are most relevant to your current practice. If you think it useful, jot down your thoughts.

How do you feel about your meditation practice?
How is your response to meditation changing over time? Is it getting better? Has it become mechanistic? Do you need to change your attitude or approach to it in some way?

Routine?
Have you been maintaining a routine practice recently? If you have drifted away from a routine, what do you need to change to get yourself back into a daily routine?

Longer sessions?
Have you engaged in any longer sessions (45 minutes or more)? If so, what was that experience like? What did you gain, or learn, from these?

Themes arising in your inner chatter?
What kinds of themes have emerged recently in your inner chatter during meditation? What do these suggest to you about your life, your study, your meditation practice?

What kind of emotional state have you been in recently?
Have you noticed a recurrence of any particular emotions recently, in meditation or outside of it? What do you think is giving rise to these? Are you able to meditate through these? Do you need to talk to anybody about what you have been feeling?

Has meditation been comfortable recently?
Do you need to change anything about your posture, your seating, your meditation space?

Are you applying mindfulness and Metta to benefit your study?	How are you making use of mindfulness and Metta, consciously, to affect your studies? How well is that working? Which aspects of your study are most challenging at the moment? Are there any further ways that you could apply mindfulness or self-kindness to help with these, or with your general approach to learning?
Application of mindfulness and Metta to everyday life?	Have you drawn on mindfulness or Metta techniques during the course of everyday interactions? What happened? How could you extend this to other situations?
Meditation with others?	Have you spent any time meditating with other people? How was that experience different from meditating alone? Is this the right group for you?
General impact on you and your life?	Have you noticed any ways that mindfulness is making a difference to you generally? Have there been any changes in the way that you think or act? Has anybody else commented on changes they have seen in you?

(d) Record of meditation time

If you wish, keep a record of how long you spend each day in Mindfulness of Breathing and Metta meditations, and other mindfulness activity such as DMM, mindful walking, everyday mindfulness, etc.

Weekly record: Dates:

Practice/Day	M	T	W	Th	F	S	Su	Week: Total minutes
Mindfulness of Breathing								
Metta								
Other								
Daily total								

Weekly record: Dates:

Practice/Day	M	T	W	Th	F	S	Su	Week: Total minutes
Mindfulness of Breathing								
Metta								
Other								
Daily total								

Weekly record: Dates:

Practice/Day	M	T	W	Th	F	S	Su	Week: Total minutes
Mindfulness of Breathing								
Metta								
Other								
Daily total								

Record of meditation time

Weekly record: Dates:

Practice/Day	M	T	W	Th	F	S	Su	Week: Total minutes
Mindfulness of Breathing								
Metta								
Other								
Daily total								

Weekly record: Dates:

Practice/Day	M	T	W	Th	F	S	Su	Week: Total minutes
Mindfulness of Breathing								
Metta								
Other								
Daily total								

Weekly record: Dates:

Practice/Day	M	T	W	Th	F	S	Su	Week: Total minutes
Mindfulness of Breathing								
Metta								
Other								
Daily total								

Record of meditation time

Weekly record: Dates:

Practice/Day	M	T	W	Th	F	S	Su	Week: Total minutes
Mindfulness of Breathing								
Metta								
Other								
Daily total								

Weekly record: Dates:

Practice/Day	M	T	W	Th	F	S	Su	Week: Total minutes
Mindfulness of Breathing								
Metta								
Other								
Daily total								

Weekly record: Dates:

Practice/Day	M	T	W	Th	F	S	Su	Week: Total minutes
Mindfulness of Breathing								
Metta								
Other								
Daily total								

Record of meditation time

Weekly record: Dates:

Practice/Day	M	T	W	Th	F	S	Su	Week: Total minutes
Mindfulness of Breathing								
Metta								
Other								
Daily total								

Weekly record: Dates:

Practice/Day	M	T	W	Th	F	S	Su	Week: Total minutes
Mindfulness of Breathing								
Metta								
Other								
Daily total								

Weekly record: Dates:

Practice/Day	M	T	W	Th	F	S	Su	Week: Total minutes
Mindfulness of Breathing								
Metta								
Other								
Daily total								

(e) Reflection on practice

The best things about my recent mindfulness and Metta practice

....

....

....

Things I have found difficult about mindfulness or Metta recently

....

....

....

Ways I have applied mindfulness and Metta to my everyday life and studies recently

....

....

....

....

Things I have learnt or gained from mindfulness and Metta recently

....

....

....

....

(f) Reflection on Deliberately Mindful Moments

Date	Time	How long it lasted

Where I was/what prompted me to take a DMM at that moment

....

....

....

What I did

....

....

What it felt like

....

....

What I observed at the time

....

....

Any observations I made later (changes in mood, in how I approached tasks, or interacted with others, etc.)

....

....

....

References and bibliography

Adler, R. F. and Benbunan-Fich, R. (2013) 'Self-interruptions in discretionary multitasking'. *Computers in Human Behavior*, 29: 1441–1449.

Allen, M., Dietz, M., Blair, K. S., van Beek, M., Rees, G., Vestergaard-Poulsen, P., Lutz, A. and Roepstorff, A. (2012) 'Cognitive-affective neural plasticity following active-controlled mindfulness intervention'. *The Journal of Neuroscience*, 32: 15601–15610.

Beddoe, A. and Murphy, S. (2004) 'Does mindfulness decrease stress and foster empathy among nursing students?' *Journal of Nursing Education*, 43(7): 305–312.

Bremner, J. D. and Narayan, M. (1998) 'The effects of stress on memory and the hippocampus throughout the life cycle: Implications for childhood development and aging'. *Development & Psychopathology*, 10: 871–885.

Brewer, J. A., Worhunsky, P. D., Gray, J. R., Tang, Y.-Y., Weber, J. and Kober, H. (2011) 'Meditation experience is associated with differences in default mode network activity and connectivity'. *Proceedings of the National Academy of Sciences*, 108: 20254–20259.

Brown, K. W. and Ryan, R. M. (2003) 'The benefits of being present: Mindfulness and its role in psychological well-being'. *Journal of Personality and Social Psychology*, 84: 822–848.

Brown, K. W., Ryan, R. M. and Creswell, J. D. (2007) 'Mindfulness: Theoretical foundations and evidence for its salutary effects'. *Psychological Inquiry*, 18: 211–237.

Buetti, S. and Lleras, A. (2016) 'Distractibility is a function of engagement, not task difficulty: Evidence from a new oculomotor capture paradigm'. *Journal of Experimental Psychology: General*, 145(10): 1382–1405.

Burak, L. (2012) 'Multitasking in the university classroom'. *International Journal for the Scholarship of Teaching and Learning*, 6(2): 1–12.

Cahn, B. R. and Polich, J. (2009) 'Meditation (Vipassana) and the P3a event-related brain potential'. *International Journal of Psychophysiology*, 72: 51–60.

Cahn, B. R., Delorme, A. and Polich, J. (2013) 'Event-related delta, theta, alpha and gamma correlates to auditory oddball processing during Vipassana meditation'. *Social Cognitive and Affective Neuroscience*, 8: 100–111.

Calderwell, C., Ackerman, P. L. and Conklin, E. M. (2014) 'What else do college students 'do' whilst studying. An investigation of multitasking'. *Computers and Education*, 75: 19–29.

Carrier, L. M., Rosen, L. D., Cheever, N. A. and Lim, A. F. (2015) 'Causes, effects and practicalities of everyday multitasking'. *Developmental Review* (doi:10.1016/j.dr.2014.12.005).

Clayson, D. E. and Haley, D. A. (2012) 'An introduction to multitasking and texting: Prevalence and impact on grades and GPA in marketing classes'. *Journal of Marketing Education*, 35(1): 26–40.

Cottrell, S. (2012) *The Exam Skills Handbook. Achieving Peak Performance* (London: Palgrave).

Cottrell, S. (2013) *The Study Skills Handbook* (London: Palgrave).

Cottrell, S. (2014) *Dissertations and Project Reports*. (London: Palgrave).

Cottrell, S. (2015) *Skills for Success: Personal Development and Employability*. (London: Palgrave).

Cottrell, S. (2017) *Critical Thinking Skills: Effective Analysis, Argument and reflection*. (London: Palgrave).

Cottrell, S. (2018 and updated annually) *The Palgrave Student Planner*. (London: Palgrave).

Davidson, R., Kabat-Zinn, J., Schumacher, J., Rosenkranz, M., Muller, D., Santorelli, S. F., Urbanowski, F., Harrington, A., Bonus, K. and Sheridan, J. F. (2003) 'Alterations in brain and immune function produced by mindfulness meditation'. *Psychosomatic Medicine*, 65: 564–570.

Deckro, G. R., Ballinger, K. M., Hoyt, M., Wilcher, M., Dusek, J., Myers, P. et al. (2002) 'The evaluation of a mind/body intervention to reduce psychological distress and perceived stress in college students'. *Journal of American College Health*, 50: 281–287.

Ding, X., Tang, Y.-Y., Cao, C., Deng, Y., Wang, Y., Xin, X. and Posner, M. I. (2015) 'Short-term meditation modulates brain activity of insight evoked with solution cue'. *Social Cognitive and Affective Neuroscience*, 10: 43–49.

Farley, J., Risko, E. F. and Kingstone, A. (2013) 'Everyday attention and lecture retention: The effects of time, fidgeting, and mind wandering'. *Frontiers in Psychology*, 4: 619.

Foerde, K., Knowlton, B. J. and Poldrack, R. (2006) 'Modulation of competing memory systems by distraction'. *Proceedings of the National Academy of Sciences*, 103:11778–11783.

Gard, T., Taquet, M., Dixit, R., Hölzel, B. K., de Montjoye, Y.-A., Brach, N., Salat, D. H., Dickerson, B. C., Gray, J. R. and Lazar, S. W. (2014) 'Fluid intelligence and brain functional organization in aging yoga and meditation practitioners'. *Frontiers in Aging Neuroscience*, 6: 76.

Good, D. J., Lyddy, C. J., Glomb, T. M., Bono, J. E., Brown, K. W., Duffy, M. K., Baer, R. A., Brewer, J. A., Lazar, S.W. (2015) 'Contemplating mindfulness at work'. *Journal of Management*, 42(1): 114–142. First published date: 19 November 2015.

Hall, P. D. (1999) 'The effect of meditation on the academic performance of African American college students'. *Journal of Black Studies*, 29(3): 408–415.

Hill, K. T. (1984) 'Debilitating motivation and testing: A major educational problem, possible solutions, and policy applications'. In P. Ames and C. Ames (eds), *Research on Motivation in Education: Student Motivation*. (New York: Academic Press), pp. 245–274.

Hölzel, B., Carmody, J., Vangel, M., Congleton, C., Yeramsetti, S. M., Gard T. and Lazar, S. W. (2011) 'Mindfulness practice leads to increases in regional brain gray matter density'. *Psychiatry Research Neuroimaging*, 191(1): 36–43.

Jain, S., Shapiro, S. L., Swanick, S., Roesch, S., Mills, P., Bell, I. and Schwartz, G. (2007) 'A randomized controlled trial of mindfulness meditation versus relaxation training: Effects on distress, positive states of mind, rumination, and distraction'. *Annals of Behavioral Medicine*, 33: 11–21.

Jha, A. P., Morrison, A. B., Dainer-Best, J., Parker, S., Rostrup, N. and Stanley, E. A. (2015) 'Minds "at attention": Mindfulness training curbs attentional lapses in military cohorts'. *PLoS ONE*, 10: e0116889.

Keogh, E., Bond, F. W. and Flaxman, P. E. (2006) 'Improving academic performance and mental health through a stress management intervention: Outcomes and mediators of change'. *Behaviour Research and Therapy*, 44: 339–357.

Kozasa, E. H., Sato, J. R., Lacerda, S. S., Barreiros, M. A., Radvany, J., Russell, T. A., Sanches, L. G., Mello, L. E. and Amaro, E. (2012) 'Meditation training increases brain efficiency in an attention task'. *Neuroimage*, 59: 745–749.

LaBerge, D. (1995) *Attentional Processing: The Brain's Art of Mindfulness* (Cambridge, MA: Harvard University Press).

Lazar, S. W., Kerr, C. E., Wasserman, R. H., Gray, J. R., Greve, D. N., Treadway, M. N., McGarvey, M., Quinn, B. T., Dusek, J. A., Benson, H., Rauch, S. L., Moore, C. I. and Fischl, B. (2005) 'Meditation experience is associated with increased cortical thickness'. *NeuroReport*, 16(17): 1893–1897.

Levine, L. E., Waite, B. M. and Bowman, L. L. (2012) 'Mobile media use, Multitasking and distractibility'. *The International Journal of Cyber Behavior, Psychology and Learning* 2(3).

Levy, D. M., Wobbrock, J. O., Kasniak, A. W. and Ostergren, M. (2012) 'The effects of mindfulness meditation training on multitasking in a high-stress information environment'. In *Proceedings-Graphics Interface*, 38th Graphics Interface Conference, GI 2012, 28–30 May (Toronto, ON, Canada), pp. 45–52.

Lindquist, S. I. and McLean, J. P. (2011) 'Daydreaming and its correlates in an educational environment'. *Learning and Individual Differences* 21(2): 158–167 (doi: 10.1016/j.lindif.2010.12.006).

Loh, K. K. and Kanai, R. (2014) 'High Media multi-tasking is associated with smaller gray-matter density in the anterior cingulate cortex'. *Plos One* (24/9/2014).

Lutz, A., Brefczynski-Lewis, J., Johnstone, T. and Davidson, R. J. (2008) 'Regulation of the neural circuitry of emotion by compassion meditation: Effects of meditative expertise'. *PLoS One*, 3(3): 1–10.

Lutz, A., Slagter, H. A., Rawlings, N. B., Francis, A. D., Greischar, L. L. and Davidson, R. J. (2009) 'Mental training enhances attentional stability: Neural and behavioral evidence'. *The Journal of Neuroscience*, 29: 13418–13427.

Mark, G., Gudith, J. and Klocke, U. (2008) 'The cost of interrupted work: More speed and stress'. *Proceedings of the SIGCHI Conference on Human Factors in Computing Systems*, pp. 107–110.

Miller, E. (2016) 'Here's why you shouldn't multitask, according to an MIT neuroscientist'. *Tools of the Trade*. At: www.fortune.com (downloaded 17/7/2017).

Mrazek, M. D., Franklin, M. S., Phillips, D. T., Baird, B. and Schooler, J. W. (2013) 'Mindfulness training improves working memory capacity and GRE performance while reducing mind wandering'. *Psychol. Sci.*, 24: 776–781 (pmid:23538911).

Narr, K. L., Woods, R. P., Thompson, P. M., Szeszko, P., Robinson, D. et al. (2007) 'Relationships between IQ and regional cortical gray matter thickness in healthy adults'. *Cerebral Cortex*, 17(9): 2163–2171.

National Union of Students [NUS] (2015) 'Mental Health Poll Nov 15'. http://appg-students.org.uk/wp-content/uploads/2016/03/Mental-Health-Poll-November-15-Summary.pdf (accessed January 2018).

Ophir, E., Nass, C. and Wagner, A. D. (2009) 'Cognitive control in media-multi-taskers'. In *Proceedings of the National Academy of Sciences of the United States of America*, 106(35): 15583–15587.

Ostafin, B. D., Kassman, K. T. (2012) 'Stepping out of history: Mindfulness improves insight problem solving'. *Consciousness and Cognition*, 21: 1031–1036.

Pagnoni, G. (2012) 'Dynamical properties of BOLD activity from the ventral posteromedial cortex associated with meditation and attentional skills'. *Journal of Neuroscience*, 32: 5242–5249.

Roeser, R. W., Schonert-Reichl, K. A., Jha, A., Cullen, M., Wallace, L., Wilensky, R., Oberle, E., Thomson, K., Taylor, C. and Harrison, J. (2013) 'Mindfulness training and reductions in teacher stress and burnout: Results from two randomized, waitlist-control field trials'. *Journal of Educational Psychology*, 105: 787–804.

Rosen, L. D., Carrier, L. M. and Cheever, N. A. (2013a) 'Facebook and texting made me do it: Media-induced task-switching while studying'. *Computers in Human Behavior*, 29: 948–958.

Rosen, L. D., Whaling, K., Rab, S., Carrier, L. M. and Cheever, N. A. (2013b) 'Is Facebook creating "iDisorders"? The link between clinical symptoms of psychiatric disorders and technology use, attitudes and anxiety'. *Computers in Human Behavior*, 29(3): 1243–1254.

Sana, F., Weston, T. and Wiseheart, M. (2013) 'Laptop multitasking hinders learning for both users and nearby peers'. *Computers and Education*, 62: 24–31.

Sayette, M. A., Schooler, J. W. and Reichle, E. D. (2010) 'Out for a smoke: The impact of cigarette craving on zoning out during reading'. *Psychol. Sci.*, 21: 26–30 (pmid:20424018).

Shapiro, S. L., Astin, J. A., Bishop, S. R. and Cordova, M. (2005) 'Mindfulness-based stress reduction for health care professionals: Results from a randomized trial'. *International Journal of Stress Management*, 12(2): 164–176.

Shapiro, S. L., Brown, K. and Biegel, G. (2007) 'Self-care for health care professionals: Effects of MBSR on mental well being of counseling psychology students'. *Training and Education in Professional Psychology*, 1: 105–115.

Shapiro, S. L., Brown, K. W. and Astin, J. A. (2008) 'Towards the integration of meditation into higher education: A review of the research'. Paper prepared for the Center for Contemplative Mind in Society, accessed from: http://prsinstitute.org/downloads/related/spiritual-sciences/meditation/TowardtheIntegrationofMeditationintoHigher Education.pdf (7/27/17).

Sharf, R. H. (2015) 'Is mindfulness Buddhist? (and why it matters)'. *Transcultural Psychiatry*, 52(4): 470–484.

Slagter, H. A., Lutz, A., Greischar, L. L., Francis, A. D., Nieuwenhuis, S., Davis, J. M. and Davidson, R. J. (2007) 'Mental training affects distribution of limited brain resources'. *PLoS Biology*, 5: e138.

Smallwood, J., Fitzgerald, A., Miles, L. K. and Phillips, L. H. (2009) 'Shifting moods, wandering minds: Negative moods lead the mind to wander'. *Emotion*, 9: 271–276 (pmid: 19348539).

Smallwood, J. and Schooler, J. W. (2015) 'The science of mind wandering: Empirically navigating the stream of consciousness'. *Annual Review of Psychology*, 66: 487–518.

Stone, L. (2009) *Beyond Simple Multi-tasking: Continuous Partial Attention* (blog article on Lindastone.net. N.p., Nov. 2009).

Suzuki, S. (1973) *Zen Mind, Beginner's Mind. Informal Talks on Zen Meditation* (New York: Weatherhill).

Sydney Morning Herald (2007) *Meditation sharpens brain*, 9 July. Retrieved from http://www.smh.com.au/news/National/Meditation-sharpens-brain-scientis ts/2007/07/09/1183833405072.html. Cited in Shapiro et al. (2008).

Tang, Y.-Y., Ma, Y., Wang, J., Fan, Y., Feng, S., Lu, Q., Yu, Q., Sui, D., Rothbart, M. K., Fan, M. and Posner, M. I. (2007) 'Short-term meditation training improves attention and self-regulation'. *Proceedings of the National Academy of Sciences*, 104: 17152–17156.

Tang, Y.-Y., Hölzel, B. K. and Posner, M. I. (2015) 'The neuroscience of mindfulness meditation'. *Nature Reviews Neuroscience*, 16: 213–225.

Taylor, C. (2011) 'For Millennials, social media is not all fun and games'. *GigaOM*, 29 April (http://gigaom.com/2011/04/29/millennial-mtv-study).

Teasdale, J. D. (1999) 'Emotional processing, three modes of mind and the prevention of relapse in depression'. *Behaviour Research and Therapy*, 37: S53–S77.

Teasdale, J., Segal, Z. V., Williams, J. M. G. and Lau, M. A. (2000) 'Prevention of relapse/recurrence in major depression by mindfulness-based cognitive therapy'. *Journal of Counseling and Clinical Psychology*, 68(4): 615–623.

Thich Nhat Hanh (1988) *The Sun My Heart: From Mindfulness to Insight Contemplation* (Berkeley, CA: Parallax Press).

Vinski, M. T. and Watter, S. (2013) 'Being a grump only makes things worse: A transactional account of acute stress on mind wandering'. *Front Psychology*, 4: 730 (pmid:24273520).

Walsh, J. P. (1995) 'Managerial and organizational cognition: Notes from a trip down memory lane'. *Organization Science*, 6: 280–321.

Willingham, D. T. (2010) 'Have technology and multitasking rewired how students learn?' In *American Educator*, 34(2): 23–28, 42 (Sum 2010).

Wilson, T.D., Reinhard, D.A., Westgate, E.C. et al. (2014) 'Just think: The challenges of the disengaged mind'. *Science*, 4 July, 345(6192): 75–77.

Wood, E., Zivcakova, L., Gentile, P., Archer, K., De Pasquale, D. and Nosko, A. (2012) 'Examining the impact of off-task multi-tasking with technology on real-time classroom learning'. *Computers and Education*, 58, 365–374.

Index

Mindfulness for study and for life

When you are studying, just study

When you are eating, just eat

When you are exercising, just exercise

When you work on an assignment, just do that

When you are at work, just focus on the job

When you are meditating, just meditate

When you are reflecting, just reflect

When you are creating something, just create

When you are messaging, just message

When you are resting, just rest

When you are revising, just revise

When you are in the exam, just focus on the exam

When you are solicializing, just socialize

When you lie down to sleep, just sleep